THE CLASSROOM SURVIVAL BOOK

A PRACTICAL MANUAL FOR TEACHERS

The Classroom Survival Book

A PRACTICAL MANUAL FOR TEACHERS

by Margaret Martin Maggs

NEW VIEWPOINTS
A DIVISION OF FRANKLIN WATTS
NEW YORK | LONDON

New Viewpoints
A Division of Franklin Watts
730 Fifth Avenue
New York, New York 10019

Library of Congress Cataloging in Publication Data

Maggs, Margaret.
The classroom survival book.

Includes index.
1. Classroom management—Handbooks, manuals, etc.
2. Teaching—Handbooks, manuals, etc. I. Title.
LB3013.M28   371.1'02   79-21365
ISBN 0-531-06372-0
ISBN 0-531-06501-4 pbk.

CONTENTS

PART THREE
DEALING WITH OTHERS
AND YOURSELF

THE CLASSROOM SURVIVAL BOOK

A PRACTICAL MANUAL FOR TEACHERS

INTRODUCTION

Survival is a bare-boned word. It is used purposely here because this book deals with your ability to survive in the classroom. Little if anything is said about that magic blend of science and performing art that is teaching. The history and theories of teaching are *already* available in the broad scope of excellent education textbooks used today in graduate and undergraduate courses. Field-based programs for prospective teachers do much to bridge the gap between the printed word and its practice. Yet the minute the classroom door shuts and the bell rings, the teacher alone with a class must face and resolve real-life problems *before* teaching can take place.

Whether you are preparing to be a teacher, or are one with some experience, you will have problems. Sometimes those problems can produce such tension that you may lose the ideas and ideals so essential to good teaching. Your problems can range from dealing with papers to dealing with oneself and others under stress. Most supervisors, although sympathetic, are busy. And most teachers are reluctant to admit (particularly to supervisors) that they simply don't know how to do many things.

The Classroom Survival Book is a "how to" book firmly based in the day-to-day reality of classroom problems. It can be used by teachers singularly or as a text for in-service or workshop courses. The emphasis of the book is on routines and practices that can set the teacher free to go about the main business of schools: educating children.

It would be impossible to thank everyone who has helped the author. There are, though, a few who must be mentioned. Thanks are due to Ed Maggs for his physical and moral support, to John and Bill Maggs for their editorial assistance, to Ms. Selma M. Lawrence for her suggestion of the title, to Brian Morrow for his criticism, to Roy Elberfeld for his suggestions, to the supportive editors, Elza Teresa Dinwiddie and Joe Krevisky, and to my fellow members of the R.C.P. car pool, Myra Rosen and Evelyn Diaz, for their advice and patience. Most of all, thanks are due to the staff of J143M, particularly the bilingual teachers and paraprofessionals who were the inspiration for this book.

Blauvelt, New York
June, 1979

HOW TO USE THIS BOOK

Although this book has very few answers, it does raise a lot of questions because its main thrust is to help you find your own answers. If this book is being used as the text in your college or workshop course, naturally your teacher will indicate what is required reading. If, on the other hand, you are using this book on your own, use it in two ways. First, read it all the way through so that you can consider the scope of practical knowledge that a teacher must have. Second, if you keep the book for reference, let it help you meet the daily challenges of your job.

Each chapter begins with Aims and a Motivation and ends with a Summary and Homework. Within each chapter you will find practice exercises. Most of these deal with what could actually happen in your classroom. Some are designed to illustrate a parallel between what occurs outside of school and within. A few refer to previous practices.

It is important that you understand that most exercises have *no* correct answers. There may be as many responses as there are people using this book. Where there may be a limited number of alternative answers or suggestions to help you complete the practice, you will be given an illustration or an example.

It is strongly recommended that you do read the entire book through before using it as a reference tool. There are three parts: Dealing with Papers, Dealing with Students, and Dealing with

Others and Yourself. While the book is sequential, it is hoped that it functions as a whole entity just as you do in the classroom. In each section there are references to other pages. Some exercises relate to later ones.

The topics chosen here for discussion are the ones that most generally concern teachers. They are probably the ones that take up time better used by teachers in actually teaching. No book, however, could possibly include all the specific problems you will face. For that reason, throughout these pages you are encouraged to look for your own personal solutions. Once you develop the habit of meeting situations in a positive way, you will be ready for whatever may come your way.

PART ONE
DEALING WITH PAPERS

CHAPTER ONE

THE WHYS AND WAYS OF ATTENDANCE

HOW NOT TO PASS THE BUCK

AIMS

1. To understand why attendance records are more important than you think.
2. To understand the methods of attendance-keeping and follow-up for your classroom and/or your homeroom.

DO NOW

List every system of attendance keeping you have observed in classrooms where you were a student.

MOTIVATION

Most teachers like to receive a salary check. Many teachers do not stop to think, however, that accurate attendance records are the basis of those salary checks.

REQUIRED READING

There are fewer children in United States public schools this year than there were last year. This fact has a direct economic impact on education because most schools are funded on a per-child basis. For example, your school's textbook fund allocation is probably based on so-many dollars for each child. You and your colleagues were hired because someone in the education hierarchy divided the number of children in your school by the "ideal" class size and arrived at the number of teachers needed by your school. State and federal funds are given to your school because there are a particular number of children who qualify for special help.

Children in school are more than just statistics. They include Ruth who never blows her nose, Carl who can't sit still, and Jackie whose shoelaces are always untied. If Ruth and Carl and Jackie and all the others were not present in your classroom, you probably wouldn't be there either.

That is why the attendance secretary or, if you're lucky, the attendance department, is inclined to look with great disfavor on the teacher whose attendance records are casual. You are messing around with the backbone of the education establishment: money.

There are all sorts of formulas for dividing educational dollars. Some use average daily attendance, some deal in actual attendance. Most formulas, though, start with the number of bodies in your classroom. Your accuracy in counting those bodies is important. The little marks you make on the records translate into chalk, pencil sharpener, books and your paycheck.

EXERCISE

Divide your gross annual pay by the number of children you teach. The next time you look at your *least* favorite student, remember how much that child is worth to you extrinsically if not in any other way.

MAIN POINT

A school's record of the student's attendance can be a legal document.

REQUIRED READING

There are other reasons for keeping accurate attendance records. A roll book is a legal document and is sometimes subpoenaed by courts. Just as you won't lie on a witness stand, don't fib on paper. It could have embarrassing ramifications. An extreme example is Teacher A who carelessly marked Dick present on the morning of his first and hopefully last foray into crime. Teacher A found this alibi difficult to explain to an irate storekeeper who easily identified Dick as the culprit. Teacher A found it even more difficult to explain to the principal.

There are other reasons for accuracy rather than the legal. Mrs. B sends Johnny to school early every morning. Unfortunately his route lies over the railroad bridge from which he has an enthralling view. This spectator sport makes him tardy four days out of five one week, but his forgetful teacher doesn't change Johnny's initial absence marks to the amended latenesses. When Mrs. B sees Johnny's report card she becomes another angry parent who believes that "they" really don't care about her son. Out of just such trivial incidents are great resentments born.

THE TOOLS OF ATTENDANCE-TAKING

1.   Pencil versus pen: Which should you use? Find out immediately. It may make a difference. One teacher was trained in another school system to do everything in pencil till month's end. Same teacher was confronted by apoplectic supervisor, pen in hand, halfway through the month. And, by the way, if you're using ink, find out which color is acceptable. You may like green, but the attendance folk could have very different tastes.

2.   Roll book: Read directions carefully, and if you don't understand them, ask questions. Don't guess. In some roll books you mark both morning and afternoon attendance. Some use one color for attendance, another for lateness or absence. There are usually letters (a, l, A,) to be written in for specific reasons. Some require absence on religious holidays to be noted as such. A word of caution: Do not be creative. People who check roll books are not appreciative of individualization.

3.   Attendance record: Many schools require both a roll book and an attendance record that is sent early each day to a particular person. This daily sheet is where you will indicate any notes received as absence excuses. Sometimes you keep the notes. Often they're attached to the record and centrally filed. Be on time with your daily attendance or be prepared for nasty notes in your mailbox. Your data may be needed for reporting reasons.

4.   Computer attendance: Some school systems have computer facilities. In this case a usual procedure will be to send the computer card of each absentee to the central office. An absence list can be printed quickly, and latecomers are directed to a desk or area where they are checked off. The computer system, while streamlining some of the paperwork, still depends basically on your accuracy.

5.   Classroom attendance records: In secondary or any other schools where children go to more than one classroom during the day, the teacher is usually required to take in-school attendance. You may use a list in a book or a card system. Remember:

   a. Do take attendance. From first grade on there are in-school "cutters." Lack of attention to this detail could catch up with you when truant George has an accident elsewhere on *your* time.
   b. It's quicker to note absences rather than those present.
   c. Don't depend on the homeroom absence list. It may not include any latecomers.
   d. You can use a student monitor to take attendance if you keep your student grades in a separate place. It's a no-no to give a student access to grades other than his or her own.

FOLLOW-UP IN ATTENDANCE-TAKING

The roll book and classroom list are not the whole of attendance. Follow-up can be just as important. Because pupil attendance is the financial lifeblood of schools, great emphasis is placed on getting absentees into the classroom. In some school systems a separate attendance office takes care of this. The office usually has record-keeping personnel who telephone or mail letters or cards to the families of absentees. In addition there are attendance teachers (the older generation knew them as "truant officers") who work on cases of habitual truancy. Beyond this office there is ordinarily a judicial Family Court back-up which in extreme cases will help families with supervision of attendance or even place the truant in another environment such as a foster or group home. Most classroom teachers have little to do with this area, but in some systems the homeroom teacher is responsible for the initial follow-through on absences.

1. You may be required to notify the family yourself when a student is absent. There may be a special form to mail. In that case fill it out accurately the first time. If you misspell the student's name, get the address wrong or copy the wrong date of absence, you are simply making time-consuming trouble for yourself. If you are expected to telephone the family, be clear on your information and on the information you need from the parent. If phone calls must be made at night because parents work, keep written track of day and whom called and ask for reimbursement of the call's cost.

2. If, in talking with a parent, you are told of a family crisis situation (death, accident), write down the information and send it to an appropriate person, probably the guidance counselor. This situation could have an effect on the child's future work or behavior in school.

3. Be alert to the child who is absent but not ill. Parents may keep children home for other reasons including fear or distrust of the school, other children, or the teacher. While this type of situation may blow over, it can also prove to be the opening gun in a home-school war. If you sense that this may be a reason for the student's absence, try to find out the details. It could have as quick a solution as the changing of the youngster's classroom seat. On the other hand, the situation may be too big for you to handle. In that case, find an appropriate person and ask for help.

4. Try to see if there is a pattern in a child's absence. If Sarah always misses Thursdays it may be that she is a family babysitter that day. Parents who encourage this should be discouraged. Most states have laws mandating attendance, so such a practice is illegal. It is also unfair to the child.

5. Remember, in communicating with parents, you are your own public relations person. Parents can be adversaries, but they shouldn't be. You can *make* them uncooperative by being bossy, aloof and brusque. That's too bad for the child, and, in the long run, you will suffer also. No one asks you to hang on a parent's every word, but if you listen carefully, you may just learn something helpful about your student. And at least you will give the impression of being interested in the child.

EXERCISE

Complete the following conversation by filling in your remarks, then read it through again. Check the word that best describes your reaction to the caller: ☐ appreciative ☐ resentful

CALLER: I'm calling about the bill you owe us.
YOU:

CALLER: You were supposed to pay it last month.
YOU:

CALLER: You have to live up to your obligations, you know.
YOU:

CALLER: Lots of people use that excuse.
YOU:

CALLER: We're turning it over to a bill collector in 5 more days.
YOU:

CALLER: Well, mail it today and don't get behind again.

SUMMARY

1. Attendance records you keep are important because they help pay for education, and they are legal documents.
2. You may have other specific responsibilities for school and classroom attendance. Learn them by asking questions.
3. Be careful and courteous in any contact with parents over attendance.

HOMEWORK

You have called Janet's mother because Janet was absent on Monday and Tuesday. In your conversation you discover that Janet won't come to school because she's afraid of a group of girls who "pick" on her outside of the school building. The girls are older and not in your class. What steps would you take to help the situation?

PERIOD NUMBER 1

	FIRST WEEK				SECOND WEEK				THIRD WEEK				FOURTH WEEK			
	MONTH				MONTH				MONTH				MONTH			
	DATE				DATE				DATE				DATE			
1																
2																
3																
4																
5																
6																
7																
8																
9																
10																
11																
12																
13																
14																
15																
16																
17																
18																
19																
20																
21																
22																
23																
24																
25																
26																
27																
28																
29																
30																
31																
32																
33																
34																
35																

NUMBER OF DAYS FROM BEGINNING OF TERM TO END OF THIS PERIOD _____
TOTAL NUMBER OF SCHOOL DAYS THIS PERIOD _____

FIFTH WEEK					SIXTH WEEK					TOTAL THIS PERIOD			TOTAL TO DATE			
MONTH					MONTH					TOTAL ATTEND.	TOTAL ABSENCE	TOTAL LATENESS	TOTAL ATTEND.	TOTAL ABSENCE	TOTAL LATENESS	
DATE					DATE											
																1
																2
																3
																4
																5
																6
																7
																8
																9
																10
																11
																12
																13
																14
																15
																16
																17
																18
																19
																20
																21
																22
																23
																24
																25
																26
																27
																28
																29
																30
																31
																32
																33
																34
																35

| | NAME OF PUPIL–BOYS (WRITE SURNAME FIRST) (LIST IN ALPHABETICAL ORDER) | DAYS ABSENT LAST YEAR | ADM. OR DISCH. | DATE OF BIRTH | | | PRESENT GRADE | FULL NAME OF PARENT OR GUARDIAN | TELEPHONE |
				MONTH	DAY	YEAR			
1									
2									
3									
4									
5									
6									
7									
8									
9									
10									
11									
12									
13									
14									
15									
16									
17									
18									
19									
20									
21									
22									
23									
24									
25									
26									
27									
28									
29									
30									
31									
32									
33									
34									
35									
	DAILY TOTALS								

School Year 1978-79 (PRINT) SCH. Current New Class Class as of 6/78

PUPIL'S NAME (Last) (First) BORO Fall Spring

Total Abs. Last Year _____

	M/F (Circle One)	BIRTH DATE				HOME PHONE	BUSINESS PHONE

Address _____ PARENT/GUARDIAN _____ Zip # _____ Apt. # _____ Teacher _____

Address _____ Zip # _____ Apt. # _____ Teacher _____

1978	M	T	W	TH	F	M	T	W	TH	F	M	T	W	TH	F	M	T	W	TH	F	M	T	W	TH	F	MAX. SCH. DAYS	ATT	ABS	LATE
SEPT					1	4	5	6	7	8	11	12	13	14	15	18	19	20	21	22	25	26	27	28	29	15			
OCT	2	3	4	5	6	9	10	11	12	13	16	17	18	19	20	23	24	25	26	27	30	31				18			
NOV			1	2	3	6	7	8	9	10	13	14	15	16	17	20	21	22	23	24	27	28	29	30		19			
DEC					1	4	5	6	7	8	11	12	13	14	15	18	19	20	21	22	25	26	27	28	29	16			
1979 JAN	1	2	3	4	5	8	9	10	11	12	15	16	17	18	19	22	23	24	25	26	29	30	31			21			
Total 1st Term																													
FEB				1	2	5	6	7	8	9	12	13	14	15	16	19	20	21	22	23	26	27	28			18			
MAR				1	2	5	6	7	8	9	12	13	14	15	16	19	20	21	22	23	26	27	28	29	30	22			
APR	2	3	4	5	6	9	10	11	12	13	16	17	18	19	20	23	24	25	26	27	30					14			
MAY		1	2	3	4	7	8	9	10	11	14	15	16	17	18	21	22	23	24	25	28	29	30	31		22			
JUNE					1	4	5	6	7	8	11	12	13	14	15	18	19	20	21	22	25	26	27	28	29	19			

PUPIL'S NAME (Last, First) I. D. # _____

DATE ADM. _____
DATE DISCH. _____
INTERCLASS _____

From _____
To _____

PROMOTED TO _____ YEAR TO DATE _____

CHAPTER TWO

REPORT CARDS AND PERMANENT RECORDS

READING AND WRITING BETWEEN THE LINES

AIMS

1. To learn how to deal with variations in the reporting of achievement to parents.
2. To learn how to read and write student permanent records.

DO NOW

Write a short paragraph (50 words or less) explaining in terms a parent can understand what the difference is between a B-plus and an A-minus. Do you understand the difference yourself?

MOTIVATION

It is the rare student who has never received an unfair grade, asked for an explanation and still not understood why. Many of us have also suffered problems with a registrar's office or mistakes on transcripts. Report cards and permanent record cards of students are only as clear and accurate as you make them.

REQUIRED READING

Education may have become an organization of recordkeepers. If so, it only reflects the world around us. Some teachers feel that time spent on paperwork is time wasted. Unfortunately, few school systems give much clerical help to teachers. It is up to you, then, to organize yourself as efficiently as possible. To do this, you must understand what is expected of you. One area that has always been a teacher responsibility is that of reporting achievement to parents, or report cards.

REPORT CARDS

There are basically two styles of reporting student achievement: symbols and words. Many systems prefer not to give students number or letter marks, at least until the secondary school. In this case the teacher must write comments on student achievement. To do so you must decide what student achievement is—improvement by itself or improvement measured against certain standards. The school system's philosophical approach has probably been mapped out already for you in a memo, circular or booklet. If it hasn't and the decision appears to be yours, discuss your attitude with a supervisor. At least know what standards you are using and why.

EXERCISE

Ellen is a quiet well-behaved child in the third grade. She began the year reading on a 1.5 level. In six months she has improved to a 2.5 level. Of course, this is still a year below grade. Is Ellen passing or failing? What can you tell her parents?

Education-ese like most jargon has the effect of excluding from understanding those people who do not speak it. It can also be defensive. The harsh fact that Kevin doesn't blow his nose enough, when translated to "inadequate health habits," breaks things so gently to the parents that they haven't the foggiest idea of what the teacher means.

You have a responsibility to tell parents what is going on with their children. This can be done clearly without insults. Avoid polysyllables. "Makes a minimal effort toward achievement" really means "Must try harder." "Neglects follow-through tasks" should be translated to "Doesn't do homework." "Has low organizational standards" means "Should do neater work." If you are responsible for written reports to parents, remember that they must understand what you say. Otherwise, why bother?

Some school systems bypass the individual teacher comment and use number codes (sometimes in connection with a computerized system) that correspond with most-used phrases. This has the effect of lightening your written work, yet it makes parent-teacher communication more impersonal and demands care in the choice of preprinted comment. You may inadvertently mark 6 ("Works to capacity") when you really meant 4 ("Must try harder"). And you may not find a comment that is really what you want to tell the parent.

When a school system uses number grades on report cards, it is likely that there are certain "understood" conventions. It is up to you to find out what restrictions there may be on grades. (In number grades 65 is usually passing. In letter grades D is passing, but barely.) Some systems use a particular grade (i.e., 40) for students who fail because of excessive absences. Some subject areas in a secondary school might have a specific type of grade for students who fail because they do not meet a subject requirement such as "dressing" for gym. Some systems permit teachers to give any appropriate number grade. Others require that marks be only in multiples of five. For marks during the school year a grade of 60 may indicate that, while failing, the student is expected to pass eventually. Some of this grading shorthand does not appear on the report card itself, and you will not know unless you ask.

When letter grades are given there may be different divisions of categories. Where an A-F system has five categories, an O-U system could have anywhere from three to five. It is important when giving letter grades to know how many divisions there are in order to judge a student's achievement accurately. Translating O to Outstanding means nothing unless you know whether this is one of three grades possible (Outstanding, Satisfactory, Unsastisfactory) or five (Outstanding, Good, Satisfactory, Unsatisfactory, Failing). If plusses and minuses are acceptable, you can get some further flexibility, but letter grades can be very arbitrary.

A student's specific conduct grade may not be your decision.

Most report cards in elementary school and in some secondary schools indicate the student's nonacademic behavior with a mark or remarks. Some systems divide this behavior into various areas such as Courtesy, Effort, Responsibility and Self-Control. (See sample permanent record card, page 26.) You may find, though, that these areas are not subject to your individual judgment. Effort, for example, may be tied to a student's passing all courses. (Never mind that he or she could be making 95, you think, and instead is in the low 70s.) Responsibility may be tied to the student's lateness, absence or homework record. Self-control may be considered adequate unless the student has been reported to an administrator for misbehavior X times during the year. Because the whole area of student behavior standards is subjective, you may be asked to justify a failing grade here more often than in an academic area. One of the best back-ups you can have is an anecdotal record of each student. This is discussed at greater length in "Behavior" (Chapter Seven).

Parents may not understand all report card information. You may not either. The modern world runs on initials. Education is no exception. Pity the poor parent who receives this information: Math 6.0 T.E. Is is good? Is it bad? Is it important? In this instance the teacher, but not the parent, knows that T.E. means Teacher Estimate and that 6.0 means a beginning 6th-grade level. While this knowledge seems highly scientifically based, its significance may be questionable.

On some report cards teachers are required to give standardized results for reading and math. If those results aren't available, the teacher must estimate. You can do so rather broadly by knowing the grade level of books the student is using. It is still a subjective judgment. Unless your supervisor orders you to do so, it might be better to omit this type of "guesstimate."

Remember, too, that standardized tests are not always above question. A student for whom English is a second language, for instance, may score very low in a reading test's vocabulary section but at an acceptable level in general comprehension. On any given day a child may score higher or lower for a variety of physical and other reasons.

Look with a jaundiced eye at any section of a report card that deals with reportage of student learnings on a non-daily classroom basis. This should never be the source of categorizing a student in your eyes or those of the parent. Be ready to explain this fact to the parent.

REMEMBER:

1. In report cards tell the parents the facts in easily understood terms.
2. The significance of number or letter grades depends on local usage and may vary according to the number of grading categories available.
3. The significance of conduct grades may also depend on local usage.
4. "Other" report card information may be subject to interpretation.

PERMANENT RECORD CARDS

Permanent record cards are student profiles. A good private detective can take the monthly record of someone's bank checks and discover a great deal about that person. So can a teacher with a student's permanent record card. While these records are centralized in some systems, in others they may be found physically within the teacher's room. A teacher is not always obligated to read student records, but they can be well worth your time. Even if it is an effort, you should attempt to go through student records thoroughly early in the year. There are several areas where you can pick up valuable information.

1. Look at the student health records (see sample, pages 28–29), and look with an interpretative eye. Particularly in the early grades, vision impairment can have an important bearing on such student achievement as reading or writing. Lack of physical growth on a yearly basis may be indicative of nutritional or other problems. Has hearing been tested, and if so, could the results be related to a student's inattentiveness? Are there any special notes that would indicate the child has had an unusual number of illnesses or a special health problem? Rosemary may really need to be excused to the bathroom an inordinate number of times.

John's asthma could be aggravated by chalk dust even though he loves being eraser monitor. Health information can translate into classroom behavior, but the connection must be made by you.

2. Look at the informational section on the student's family. You may learn whether the pupil is an only, oldest, youngest, middle or one child of many. Pay attention to the address or addresses. Has the family moved often? Is this a one-parent family? Is there another language in the home? The answers to these questions can also affect day-to-day classroom dealings.

3. Look at the absence and lateness records for previous years. First, look for consistency. Breaks in a pattern could indicate a serious illness, a school or a family problem. Second, look for frequency. The information could help you be alert to a possible truant or habitual latecomer.

4. Look at the birth date. Students in one classroom may have a two-year range in age, all the way from the holdover to the student who entered school younger. One of your "babies" in the classroom may not be emotionally but chronologically immature. The younger student may also be less mature physically with a resulting influence on eye-hand coordination and dexterity.

5. Look at the classroom record in two different ways. First, check progress from year to year. Has the student always been promoted? If not, was that the year when there were many absences? Has the student remained in the same class all year or do you see evidence of frequent class changes? Second, check yearly progress in skills or subject areas. This reporting may also include teacher comments that could be useful to you.

6. Look at all material in the student's record. One standardized test may be open to question but several over a period of time will at least give you a "feel" for achievement. There may be a record of reading skills mastered, handy for you in initial reading placement. There may be a "group" I.Q. test, useful in a broad sense although you will always take its results with a grain of teacherly salt. An "individual" I.Q. test result may be more accurate, but it too is open to interpretation because of such things as cultural diversity. There may be a record of student hobbies, interests, or out-of-school activities which could give you specific ideas for motivation of lessons.

EXERCISE

Devise at least three ways you can help Aline read better with the following information from her permanent records:

1. The oldest of three children, mother living, Hungarian spoken in home.
2. Needs glasses, tall for age, among youngest in class.
3. Usually passes in reading but previous teachers indicate that she should work harder on comprehension.
4. Tests indicate that she was reading on grade level in past but more recently has slipped to somewhat below grade level.
5. Outside of school she is interested in cooking, babysitting, and swimming.

Permanent records should be updated at least once during the year to save you end-term work.

Time is the teacher's enemy and ally. With records it can be either according to your planning for its use. May and June usually find either teachers elbow deep in papers. If you can get ahead of that final flurry in any small way, you should. Some of the updating of permanent records can be done during the year. Make it a policy to check addresses and telephone numbers around February. When test results arrive, don't put them aside; take a free period and enter them. Update children's interests or hobbies after Easter vacation. Hearing or eye test results shouldn't gather dust in your desk. If you do a little bit now and then throughout the year, life will seem less dreary on the school's 180th day. Besides, with less pressure you will probably be more accurate. Both your students and next year's teachers deserve correct information.

SUMMARY

1. Student permanent record cards are an important source of information.
2. Your responsibilities for permanent records can be discharged throughout the school year as data becomes available.

HOMEWORK

1. Write a short paragraph to explain to yourself what kinds of grading you prefer and why.
2. Look in a local classified phone directory for the name and address of a large credit information bureau. Write to them and ask for your file. Check its accuracy. Remember, this information is permanently available to a wide variety of people.

SECONDARY SCHOOL – PUPIL PERMANENT RECORD CARD

PUPIL'S NAME — FAMILY NAME — GIVEN NAME

FATHER'S NAME

MOTHER'S MAIDEN NAME

OLDER BROTHER   OLDER SISTER

YOUNGER BROTHER   YOUNGER SISTER

GUARDIAN

ADDRESS

PHOTOGRAPH

YEARS IN GRADES 1-6   CIRCLE ONE
5   6   7   8

TRANSCRIPT SENT TO   DATE

ADMISSIONS–TRANSFERS–DISCHARGES

DATE	FROM	TO	REASON	ATTENDANCE TO DATE	
				PRES.	ABS.	LATE

DATE	HONORS AND AWARDS	ACTIVITIES	TERM ENDING	ADVISER	RATING

SCHOOL GUIDANCE COUNSELOR J.H.S.

SCHOOL GUIDANCE COUNSELOR H.S.

SCHOOL GUIDANCE COUNSELOR H.S.

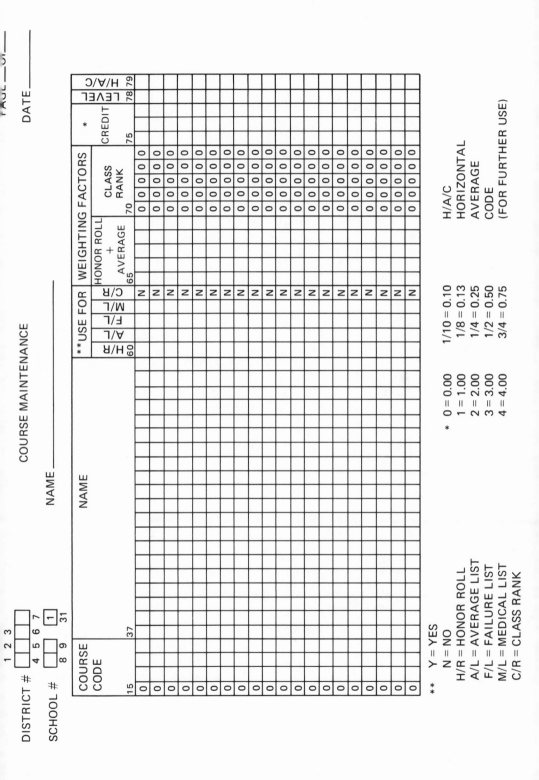

COURSE MAINTENANCE

DATE _____

DISTRICT # (1 2 3)

NAME _____

SCHOOL # (4 5 6 7) (8 9) (1 31)

COURSE CODE	NAME			**USE FOR					WEIGHTING FACTORS			*		
				H/R 60	A/L	F/L	M/L	C/R	HONOR ROLL + AVERAGE 65	CLASS RANK 70	CREDIT 75	LEVEL 78	H/A/C 79
15	37									0 0 0			

** Y = YES
   N = NO
   H/R = HONOR ROLL
   A/L = AVERAGE LIST
   F/L = FAILURE LIST
   M/L = MEDICAL LIST
   C/R = CLASS RANK

* 0 = 0.00   1/10 = 0.10
  1 = 1.00   1/8 = 0.13
  2 = 2.00   1/4 = 0.25
  3 = 3.00   1/2 = 0.50
  4 = 4.00   3/4 = 0.75

H/A/C
HORIZONTAL
AVERAGE
CODE
(FOR FURTHER USE)

CUMULATIVE HEALTH RECORD

LAST NAME (Print)	FIRST		MIDDLE				DATE OF BIRTH		
							Mo.	Day	Year

Immunizations (give date of injections)	1st	2nd	3rd	4th	5th
Smallpox					
Diphtheria–Tetanus					
Poliomyelitis					
Class					
Date (Month and Year)					
School					
Boro					
Height (in inches)					
Weight (in pounds)					
Vision with glasses — Right Eye					
Vision with glasses — Left Eye					
Vision with glasses — Both Eyes					
Vision without glasses — Right Eye					
Vision without glasses — Left Eye					
Vision without glasses — Both Eyes					
Hearing Score Screening — Right Ear					
Hearing Score Screening — Left Ear					
Hearing Score Pure Tone — Right Ear					
Hearing Score Pure Tone — Left Ear					
* Teeth					

* Code
√ Dental Certificate Issued

√		√		√		√
	T-Under Treatment	T	OK-No Treatment Needed	O K	C-Corrected	T C

Code for Teacher's Observation: √–Observed   X–No longer observed

Category	Symptom
GENERAL	Loss or no gain in weight
	Very fat
	Appears not well
	Tires easily
	Pallor
	Poor co-ordination
	Poor posture
	Pains in joints
EYES	Styes or crusted lids
	Crossed eyes
	Muscle imbalance
	Frequent headaches
	Squinting
EARS	Discharge
	Earaches
	Fails to hear questions
NOSE & THROAT	Mouth breathing
	Frequent sore throats
	Recurrent colds
	Frequent nose bleeds
NERVOUS SYMPTOMS	Difficulty in School adjustment
	Speech defect
	Nervous-restless
	Twitching movements
	Nail biting
	Excessive use of lavatory
NO. OF DAYS ABSENT FOR ILLNESS IN WRITE IN CAUSES	

CHAPTER THREE

LESSON AND UNIT PLANS

IF THIS IS TUESDAY
WE MUST BE ON PAGE 43

AIMS

1. To learn how to save time and energy in planning lessons.
2. To understand various ways of lesson-plan keeping.

DO NOW

Think of your most recent experience as a student and decide which of your teachers taught you most effectively. Were you ever aware that a lesson plan was being followed? How did you discern the teacher's organization, if any?

MOTIVATION

Some people just naturally seem to have white teeth, shiny hair, and a pleasant air although most mortals find that toothpaste, shampoo and cologne rarely keep advertised promises. Some teachers just naturally seem to have well-organized lessons while the rest of us struggle with the daily demand of "What do I do after the bell rings?" There has to be a better way.

LESSON PLANS

The first thing you need to know about lesson plans is that there is absolutely no perfect format. You may have a supervisor who feels that the ideal has been attained. If so, use that form but keep tucked away in your mind the fact that there can be many roads to success. Most forms, though, have certain common elements. They are, simply, a beginning, a middle and an end.

The beginning of a lesson plan lies within you. You must decide its purpose. But that purpose is not to teach something. Your aim is that the students learn. They may learn a process or they may learn information. You must begin your plan by asking what they should learn. The answer to that question is where you start. You usually continue this beginning with something that will show the students why they should learn what you want them to. This is called the motivation.

Once you have established your aim(s) and your motivation, you get down to the nitty-gritty of planning how to teach to accomplish those aims. You do this through talking, reading, discussion, demonstration, and questioning. The specifics depend on your subject, the students, and the time available.

If it is a long lesson you will plan to pause in the middle to summarize. At the end you will certainly sum up what has been covered. Again at the end you will do something to see if the students have learned what you hoped. This is homework, also known in the ed biz as reinforcement.

Lesson plans can be traps for the unwary. You have probably seen teachers who write minute-by-minute pages-long plans. Others scribble a few notes on the back of an envelope. How detailed your lesson plan should be is not a matter of conscience but common sense. If it tells you where you want to go and generally how to get there, it has served its purpose as your guide.

THE UNIT PLAN

The lesson plan is your daily preparation. What is the unit plan — your weekly plan? Maybe, but it's dangerous to think of a unit as always covering a specific amount of time. A unit might require two or twenty class periods. The determining factor here has to be the particular knowledge of process or information that "goes together." In this book, for instance, each chapter is concerned with a specific need for information or process knowledge by the classroom teacher. Some chapters are longer than others because of necessity.

Which comes first, the lesson plan or the unit? It is easier to take apart a jigsaw puzzle than to put it together. Many teachers unfortunately become so consumed with their daily work that they neglect overall planning. This is true not only in terms of units but of the course itself. That is probably why teachers feel that the text is the answer.

A book is not a course. Neither is the reverse true. And a teacher's manual for a book is no substitute for your own planning. Beware the lure of believing that you are teaching if you start at the beginning of the text and go to the end by the last day of class. Easy as it may seem, if you succumb to just "following the book" you are not only abdicating your freedom as a teacher, but you are shortchanging your students. Life is a variety of experiences, and the classroom is a part of life. No book can possibly account for all your needs and those of your students.

THE TIME LINE

Some teachers cling to the book simply because it is an organized long-term product. This is really too bad. You can make your own long-term organization which will probably save you time since it can serve as your own road map through the school year. You do this by using something borrowed from business—the time line. This is a rather high-class name for a simple time chart to serve as a guide to more specific planning.

You construct a time line by the initial process you use in planning a lesson. This time, though, you think in terms of what you want your students to learn by the end of the course. This may have been done partially for you by a curriculum guide or a course of study. But beware of accepting something general for the specifics of your classroom. Try to think of your aims in terms of your own knowledge and your students.

Once your aims are determined you should establish their time priority. It is quite possible that everything you do in the course has one overall purpose, such as development of reading skills. In addition, however, you will have subsidiary aims which can be fulfilled in less than the full course length. Which of these comes first, and how long will it take you to accomplish it?

Now draw a line that represents the time you have in which to accomplish everything. Indicate by crosshatches the beginning of every month. Decide which aims you will try to fulfill over what period of time. You will have something like the diagrams shown on pages 34–38.

How does this help you? In several time-saving ways. First, you now have some idea of the current aims when you sit down to write your lesson plans for a particular week. Second, you know how your present aims fit into the course-long plan. And third, you will have some organization against which you can measure the reality of the day-by-day classroom. If you like, the aims may be further developed into units that fulfill those aims.

It is quite likely that you will want to revise your time line at least once during the course. Current detours are rarely indicated on most maps. Yet this procedure can help you chart and rechart the future because it keeps your destination in mind at all times.

EXERCISE

You must teach a year-long course in Human Survival. Decide the students' grade level and list at least five aims. Use them to devise a time line.

PERSERVING YOUR LESSON PLANS

There are mystiques in all forms of creativity, and teaching is creative. A writer has a favorite pen without which he cannot work. A painter's palette must be arranged just so. Some teachers prefer preprinted lesson plan books, others like stenographer's notebooks, still others prefer a loose-leaf. Whatever your favorite, do use something permanent. You cheat yourself when you do not have a means of centralizing your lesson plans.

At one time or another you are going to be asked for your lesson plan book. It is not unknown for some teachers to spend the weekend writing backdated lesson plans from scraps of papers to show their supervisors. The less unnecessary work

ESL GRADE OR CLASS March 6-11

SUBJECT, CLASS OR SECTION

	7c		8c	6c
MONDAY	Aim: Learn how to discriminate between short o & short a aurally. Motivation: Pic SS tchr Quote "Elena, bring me the mop." "What is she asking?" Dictation: 2 col (o vs. a): rot, pat, lot, tot, cat,	sat, bat, fat, hot, pop. Review: on Board. Start: Ditto #3, same words in sentences for rat, pot, cot, shop, cap, cop, tap, top, pat, hat	Same. Add Ditto #3A: word search with o & a. NOTE: OK, but difficult concept	Same, but do Ditto 3 with class. Begin H.W in class. Do 3 sentences w/student volunteers
TUESDAY	Aim: Learn how to discriminate between short i & long e. Motivation: Pic of family in apt. Question: Are they leaving or living? Dictation: 2 col. (i vs. e): live, seek, reap,	trip, fleet, ship, steep, whip, deep, chip. Review: Board. Seatwork: Ditto #4, same in sentences. H.W: Sentences for: reap, shop, rip, dip, sick, leave, heap, lip, live, sheet	Same. Add Ditto #4A: Scram...'ed words with i & e	See above. NOTE: Better than yesterday.

WEDNESDAY	_Aim:_ Review of previous discrimination. (ŏ vs. ă & ĭ vs. ē) _Motivation:_ Tape recorder. Teacher reading. Students must mark # of ē's heard. Keep my map. Melanie take it from the ship & rip it all up	I'll use a new sheet. Discussion & replay of tape. Review of o vs.a, i vs. e: Board: pot, pat, pit, peat _Dictation:_ sound alikes 1. pot·pot pot·pat 2. live·leave live·live 3. ship·ship ship·sheep 4. tot·tot tot·tat 5. sick·seek seek·seek	"Word List: Ditto 5 Pronounce & meaning HW: Study for test _8c:_ Same: Add Dictation 6. weep·weep whip·weep 7. sick·sick sick·seek 8. lip·leap lip·lip 9. flit·flit flit·fleet 10. heap·heap hip·heap	_6c:_ Same as 7c, Ditto #5, ask only 10 words in test _NOTE:_ Need more examples.
THURSDAY	_Aim:_ Prove learning of aural discrimination _Test:_ Ditto Test #3 If time, review		_8c:_ Same. Add Ditto Test #3A	_6c:_ Same as 7c – Try anyway
FRIDAY	_Aim:_ to learn that paragraph has 1 central idea _Motivation:_ Read para. from SS book. Ask what it is saying. Ditto #6: 2 paras. Mult choice selection of central idea.	Ditto #7: 2 paras. w/out central idea Mult choice sentence of sentences. HW: Ditto #8: 4 paras w/out central idea sentences. Mult. choice.	_8c:_ Add Ditto #8: SS para similar to motivation but w/sentence missing. Class discussion of what missing sentence is.	_6c:_ Same. Begin HW in class. Do first para in class & discuss _NOTE:_ 7th did better than 8th. Why?

March 9

Science 8

Aim: To apply "weather principles" to
personal experience

Motivation: Show barometer & thermometer &
ask for difference between them.
What effect does our reading of
their information have on our lives?

Discussion: Elicit 5 principles re weather
from students as studied. Elicit
from students an example in their
terms of each. Get them to notice:
fog on river, moisture inside windows,
breath in winter, smoke rising when
air is still, etc.

Review: Quick quiz. Use weather principles
listed. Erase key words (warm,
altitude, etc.) Ask to supply them.
Students check own paper.

Homework: Must be done in morning before
school. Listen to A.M. weather forecast.
Write at least 3 effects weather will
have on your life today.

NOTE: A little bit thin. Could use another
activity

Social Studies (Grade 5)
March 9:
Aims: 1) to be able to identify well-
known patriots of early America
2) to use text to locate details

Motivation: Picture of signing of
Declaration of Independence.
Elicit answers to: Who are
these men? What do you think
they were doing? What were
they really like?

Text: To students: find names of
patriots between pages 184 and
204. List them. (10 minutes
skimming) Check answers.
Who were they? List on board:
1. Boston lawyer, second patriot
2. Minuteman leader, first to
sign Declaration
3. Commander-in-Chief, first president
4. Said, "Give me Liberty or give
me death."
5. Naval man, won important
sea battle

6. Journalist in Boston, organized
   Minutemen
7. Chief author of Declaration,
   3rd president
8. Inventor, writer, statesman,
   helped write Declaration &
   Constitution
9 & 10. Men who rode Boston to
   Lexington to warn Minutemen
Have students match description
w/person & use page no. as reference.
Check

Discussion: Which of patriots appeals
   to you personally & why?

Project developement: Students
   divide into groups to study
   one patriot. Discussion of how
   to research.

Homework: Write three specific
   questions for which you will
   try to find answers in
   library tomorrow.

NOTE: Too long - Could use two
   days for this in future.

you must do the better. If you always keep your lesson plans in one place, they are immediately available not only to you but to others.

Supervisors are not the only others who may need your plan book. Even if a substitute does not use your lesson plans, there will be at least a chance of some kind of continuity for the class when your plan book is there although you are not. Some teachers go even further and have a standby plan for substitutes clipped in the book itself.

There is a third reason for having some sort of lesson plan book, and it has to do with your students. If you want them to be organized in their approach to schoolwork, you should demonstrate to them that you too are organized. Can we expect more from them than from ourselves?

EXERCISE

Check through the sample plans in this chapter. Decide which type of lesson plan book fits you best. Then go out and buy it. Now.

ADAPTING PLANS

If one teacher with five classes writes one lesson plan in 30 minutes, how long will it take five teachers to write lesson plans for 25 classes? Perhaps not as long as you think. A teacher may write one lesson plan for five classes. That same teacher will be making a mistake, however, in thinking that all five classes will use the same material in the same way.

A lesson plan is reusable, but only with adaptations. An experienced teacher may be able to adapt instantly. It is more likely that you will want to plan your changes before you get in the classroom. How you do this is your choice. Some people write the basic lesson plan, then list each class with specific notes. Others note differences while writing the lesson plan itself.

What kind of adaptations are necessary? Perhaps one class responds well to discussion so you will spend more time on that aspect of the lesson. Perhaps another class needs work with a specific reading skill such as the finding of details, so your focus will move from discussion to text use. Perhaps the motivation you are using for other classes will not serve in a particular one. Perhaps one of the classes is advanced and needs more work provided in the same time.

Along with adaptation possibilities, you should also be alert to the strengths and weaknesses of a particular lesson plan after you have used it. Take five minutes at the end of a day and write your own comments after your plans. Be succinct but specific: "Need narrower aims," "Successful with the brightest," "More discussion questions." You may want to use part or all of this plan another time. Your own evaluation will help you decide just how it can be utilized. And if you use this technique over the school year, you will find some common threads among your successes and your failures. Those threads make up the tapestry of your teaching wisdom. (See NOTES in this chapter's sample lesson plans.)

Even success oft-repeated can become boring. Life is a series of contrasts. Whether you like it or not, so will your classroom be a place of ups and downs. Your job as a teacher is not to try and control these swings (you can't), but to take advantage of them. Plan for them.

Whether you believe it is because of biorhythms, air pressure, the phases of the moon or astrology, it is an observable fact that there are some days even in the dead of winter when "spring fever" strikes most inhabitants of a classroom. You may have a group of students who have been scaling unforeseen learning heights, yet one day you observe a glazed look in every eye and your most discussion-provoking question is met with an uneasy silence. Or it may not be the class, it may be you, an even more frightening phenomenon. You may pause five minutes into the lesson and suddenly be struck with those age-old misgivings, "What am I doing here? Am I doing anything except talking to myself? Where am I going?"

Don't despair. Be prepared. Be ready to do something absolutely different. It is the one thing that will shake you and/or your students out of the doldrums. Be courageous. Be creative. Put aside your carefully-wrought plan for the day and bring out your secret weapon, the change-of-pace lesson.

THE CHANGE-OF-PACE LESSON

Here your time line will have helped you. For each aim of the course you will have devised at least one change-of-pace lesson. It will be unusual, unexpected, maybe even zany. It could involve role playing, randomly-chosen task slips, a physical change (of seat, position or classroom). In a math class it might be a living abacus with students acting as the beads. In a second language class it might be a lesson on the music of the culture with tape recorder or songbooks. In an English class it could be your reading the most exciting part of a story of which you are very fond and then offering to lend the book to a student. In a science class it could be a walk around the school block to observe whatever fits with your course (seasonal changes, uses of electricity, sound). In social studies it might be the designing of an imaginary utopia in terms of geography, customs, politics. In most process-teaching subjects such as home economics, shop, gym, music, and art, these times will arise less frequently. There too, though, you can be prepared with a change of pace. Instead of the doing itself, students can analyze what they are doing, i.e., write instructions, evaluate new designs.

Change-of-pace lessons can be highly useful, but be careful. They can trap you also. Make sure that what the students are doing fits with your overall aim. And see to it that this change of pace is really just that. Don't continue for more than another day. Otherwise the future effectiveness of this type of lesson is lost.

EXERCISE

Take the time line you devised for the course on Human Survival. Write a brief change-of-pace plan for each of your five aims. Be realistic in terms of material available to you in the classroom, but let that be your only limit.

GET THROUGH MARCH, AND
YOU WILL LIVE TILL JUNE

"Yesterday it snowed, sleeted, rained and hailed. I have a cold sore. Mr. Hall has asked for my lesson plan book for the second time in a month. I have a bad cough that may turn into pneumonia. My favorite student is transferring out. I think I'm going to have to pay extra when I file my income tax. My life is bad enough, but I have the feeling it's going to get worse."

In terms of your day-by-day planning, you will find that by March the drear-and-drudge syndrome will have caught up with you. Although calendars do not indicate it, March contains the largest number of long school days in psychological terms. There will come one of those days when you look at your lesson plan book and despair. You have come to the end of the line.

This is a temporary condition, luckily. If you have followed the advice of this unit, you will have at least two things working to help you get yourself and your planning together. First, you have your time line so that you know generally where you should be and where you are going. Second, you have all those brief comments made at the end of each day, evaluating your lesson plans. Look back at them, particularly the ones in the beginning of the year when you were fresh as an August daisy. The type of lesson plan that worked for you then can work for you now.

Without realizing it, we tend to fall into teaching patterns. Aside from the change-of-pace lesson, you may really need to change your teaching approach. Find something you did previously (a technique, a different use of material) and forgot about. Perhaps it was not even a success but could have been, you think, with a slight difference. Ask yourself questions about the way you are teaching, and be honest in your answers. Is lecture the best way for you, your students and your subject? Is discussion? Is there really a best way or are there several better ones?

When you are overcome with that pre-spring hopelessness, don't give up. Try to learn from it.

SUMMARY

1. Write your lesson plans for yourself, making sure that they have logical beginnings, middles and ends.
2. Know where you're going in your course. Make a time line of aims.

3. Centralize lesson plans.
4. Adapt lesson plans to various classes. Analyze their strengths and weaknesses.
5. Be prepared with change-of-pace lessons.
6. If you get bogged down partway through the year, use past experience to get yourself going again.

HOMEWORK

In the lesson plan book you have bought, clip all material you put together on the Human Survival course. Refer to it before you write your next lesson plans.

CHAPTER FOUR

TESTS AND MEASUREMENTS

THE PAINLESS EXAMINATION

AIMS

1. To learn how to construct appropriate tests.
2. To learn how to give tests in the classroom.

DO NOW

Predict the student rate of success in a test with the following directions for fifth grade English: "Find 5 nouns in Column A that match 5 pronouns in Column B."

MOTIVATION

Think of the last exam you took. Was it fair? How could it have been fairer?

REQUIRED READING

In education there is a familiar saying to the effect that tests measure the teacher as well as the students. This of course means that the tests show the teacher whether the students have learned what they should. Yet a teacher can be convinced that pupils have the knowledge and the class will still "fail" the test. The answer may well lie in the test itself.

First, students need to know how to take a test. Foreign-born students from a system which concentrates on the essay test are flabbergasted by the "objective" type of exam. Pupils used to writing answers on test papers are confused when asked to use a separate answer sheet. It is your responsibility to train your students in test taking.

It is also your responsibility to construct tests that have clear instructions. In the sample, the instructions are unclear. How does the student "match" the nouns and pronouns—by drawing lines, writing letters, writing numbers? And does the teacher expect a fifth grade student to understand that the noun *student* goes with the pronoun *I* and the noun *teacher* goes with the pronoun *you?* Either noun could just as easily match *he* or *she.*

Finally, it is your responsibility to be sure that you are really testing to see whether students have understood the specific information or processes which you think they should have acquired. If you have been clear in your own mind about planning your teaching aims or objectives, then you will know what to test.

You should accustom students to tests by giving them frequently in varying ways and lengths.

THE REVIEW QUIZ

In educational semantics a quiz is shorter than an exam, and a test can be either. You can construct an oral quiz or a paper-and-pencil one. Many times students grade their own or their neighbor's quiz paper. There is usually only one kind of question, and the material is limited to what was learned in the immediate past.

Vary your use of the quiz. Don't always give it at the beginning or end of a class period. Since its purpose is to show you and your pupils any gaps in recent learning, don't emphasize individual results. It should not matter that Catherine made 100 and Jeanie 90. It is what Jeanie and the others missed that is important.

Vary your type of quiz. If you have given several true-false ones, try a short answer or a multiple-choice. In multiple-choice use letters one time and numbers another. If directions are given orally, break them down into logical steps and give children time enough to complete each step before going on. Wait till they have finished numbers from 1 to 10 before you begin explaining what they do next. If lists are placed on the board, be sure to say whether the lists are to be copied or simply used for reference. Watch yourself and the children for any misunderstanding. These misunderstandings could be multiplied in a longer test.

EXERCISE

Devise three brief quizzes to test the following learning:

"The cell is the fundamental unit of structure in living organisms. The living material is referred to as protoplasm. It can be differentiated into cytoplasm, nucleus and plasma membrane."

Have someone else take your quizzes, following directions exactly.

THE WEEKLY TEST

The weekly test is an expansion of the quiz idea. It has been carried to an extreme level of formality by English teachers. Which of us has not taken the weekly spelling test at least one year of our lives? Many teachers write only four lesson plans for a five-day week since they and their students know that Friday is Take-the-test-and-check-it Day. This unfailing rhythm has such a soothing security about it that an end-of-the-week teacher absence results in confusion.

This is all very well, but it may be unnecessary. Your subject or your students may not need a test every week. Just because it imposes organization or all the other teachers do it is not reason enough to stick to such a rigid schedule. Neither is the reverse true. There are hazards in going too long without a checkup on learning. You may be teaching only the children in the first three rows.

It is probably safe to say that a longer test than a quiz should be given at least once every ten days. In that time you should have covered enough material to form the basis of several quizzes. Whereas a quiz may have three to five questions, your test will probably run from 20 to 25. It's easier to grade, by the way, if you stay with a number that divides easily into 100.

The test should have at least two parts in it. Here is another chance for you to give children experience in varied types of test-taking. You may also want to double-check learning by asking for the same information in more than one way. Be careful, though, not to give information unintentionally in one section that you will be testing in another.

While quizzes may often be dictated or written on the board, it is most likely that your longer test will be a duplicated one. Begin to accustom students to the use of answer sheets by having them write on their own papers rather than on the test paper itself. When you do this, try to see that all answer papers are uniform. One way is to have students fold papers in half lengthwise and number according to your instructions before they begin the test. You will find this helps speed your grading.

Number your longer tests instead of dating them. If students do not mark on test papers, they can be used by several classes. In addition, you will be able to quickly identify any "missed" tests for an absentee student by using the test numbers in your grade book.

EXERCISE

"Both coffee and tea contain caffeine." Write test questions covering this information in the following ways: multiple-choice, completion, matching, true-false, short answer.

THE UNIT TEST

The term *unit* indicates a fairly hefty chunk of learning. Even if your material does not easily fall into shorter test spans, you will definitely want to test learning after a unit of work. Since the unit does cover a lot, this will be a longer test. Its length will probably be determined by class time available. You will want to write a test that can be completed within one period. This could range in length from 20 to 50 questions.

In the unit test you will have several parts. Here too you may want sections that might not be appropriate on a shorter test. Depending on the age group of students, you may have a short essay or guided composition section. Depending on the type of material, you may have a reading part where students will be required to answer questions from a prepared paragraph or several paragraphs.

Since a unit test involves more grading for you, it is most likely that you will want to use a standard answer sheet, duplicated at the same time as the test. You will, of course, leave plenty of room or give out composition paper for any written part.

In a unit test, as in longer exams, you will want questions to be "easy," others "difficult," and others "average." The usual proportion of easy to average to difficult questions is roughly a third each. You may also allow for differences in student ability by having extra credit questions or tasks.

If you plan an essay or compositon within the unit test, take into account the grade level and type of student with whom you are working. Some students may be able to write in an organized, informative way based upon instructions to define or discuss a broad-based theme with certain specifics indicated. ("Develop at least three contrasts between your choice of poets, one from the Age of Reason, the other a Romantic.") Others may need guiding, such as a sequence of questions whose answers will produce a coherent passage on the material or process learned. (See sample test on pages 54 and 55.)

In grading a composition within the unit test, have preset standards understood by the students. If you feel that form is important, make sure pupils know that they will be marked on spelling, punctuation, sentence structure, and capitalization. If this is only part of what you expect, decide how you will allocate points before you begin grading. You will not be tempted then to excuse or abuse any particular student's faults.

EXERCISE

Write the instructions for a guided composition inside a unit test of students on a particular grade level that you choose. The guided composition will answer the questions you pose on Human Beings and Their World.

MIDTERMS AND FINAL EXAMS

These are the biggies of the school year, and they occur with increasing frequency as the student progresses from late elementary to secondary school. The exams are meant to cover a half or whole year of learning. Many secondary schools have special schedules so that students may spend between an hour and a half and two hours on each exam.

These exams may be uniform in each subject area. All the students in tenth-year social studies, for example, will take the same exam. Some school systems devise exams to be used throughout all schools for a particular level and subject area.

If you are involved in writing a midterm or final exam for a particular level or subject, don't panic. It is not any more difficult than writing the shorter unit test.

First, decide specifically what should have been learned in the course. Next, devise the different types of questions you will have. There will probably be at least five parts to the exam. Try to vary the parts to cover the range available to you. Assign importance to each part in terms of its percentage of the whole test. Keep that percentage in mind when you write the specific questions of a part so that the point value of each answer is easily calculated. Once you have written your questions, add instructions. Construct an answer sheet to go with the test paper. And in making up your answer key, read through the test carefully for mechanical and psychological errors.

EXERCISE

You must write a midterm exam for eleventh-grade American history. You will be covering the colonial period, the American Revolution, westward expansion, and the Civil War between the States. Write an outline of six parts to the exam with their percentage value. Write a sample question for each part.

The act of giving a test can be as important to student success as the making of the test.

Your responsibility as a teacher is both day-to-day and long-term. Part of the long-term effect you can have on your students lies in the mental preparation you give them for tests. Certainly you will train pupils to follow instructions and to take different kinds of tests. In addition, however, you will need to show them how to prepare themselves.

One logical way to show your students how to study for tests is to give them review sheets, covering material to be tested. Some teachers go even further and have each student prepare his or her own review. This can be done with outlines that the student fills in or a logical sequence of questions that the student answers. You will not, of course, give the same questions in the same way that they appear on the test.

You need to tell your students what materials they will need in order to take the test. Some tests require pens, others pencils. Some tests are open-book, in which case the student will need the text. In areas such as drafting or math there may be special instruments needed. Sometimes pupils supply paper. Other times teachers prefer that test takers bring nothing into the classroom. Be clear in your instructions to the class before the test day itself.

Probably the most important pretest responsibility you have, though, is to make clear to your students why they are taking the test. Tests are important but sometimes that importance looms so large to the student that results become skewed. You will probably have at least one student who knows the test material but is so concerned about it that he or she forgets everything. You will probably have at least one student who is so concerned about passing that he or she will cheat. Face these facts in your own mind and deal with them in class before the test day.

What should you do about the student who goes to pieces? That is your decision. Remember that if you offer the student a second chance you must do so for everyone in the class. What do you do about the test taker who cheats? That is also up to you, but make your decision before the test and stick to it for everyone. Remember that you may have to justify any action not only to supervisors and parents but to yourself.

EXERCISE

Next Thursday you are giving your class a unit test. Today you will tell them what the test will be like and what rules you will have for them during the test. What will you say?

GIVING THE TEST

A breathless hush falls across the room. The moment of truth has arrived. Look around that room and ask yourself some quick questions before you hand out the test papers.

First, do your students have enough elbow room? If you can move desks or people apart, it will be easier for everyone. Someone who is a slow test taker can get very nervous next to a whizzer. Eyes stray without meaning to do so. Someone sighing next to you does nothing for your own morale. Don't hesitate to move students around for a test. It is to everyone's advantage.

Do your students know what to expect of you? Have you made clear the procedure in everything from cheating to a bomb scare? Do they know to raise a hand for help instead of getting up? Have you told them that the early finishers should go back and double-check every answer? Only if you are sure that there are no more questions should you begin handing out the papers.

When you hand out papers, do it efficiently. Some teachers begin in the back of the room and walk backwards to the front, placing the test blank side up till everyone has a copy and all can begin at once. Others prefer to pass the required number to the back by student monitors while supervising from the front. You may want to have students pass papers across the room. Whatever you decide, distribute papers quickly. There is no point in keeping students on tenterhooks in an already tense situation.

During the test, don't catch up on the crossword puzzle. Even when no one appears to need help, walk quietly around the room. Stand in the back for a while. You get a whole different perspective. Watch which questions give which students the most difficulty. See if instructions are being followed correctly. Maybe they aren't as clear as you thought. If a student points out an error, correct it on the blackboard and draw everyone's attention to it.

EXERCISE

You are giving a unit test to a third-grade class. Ten minutes into the test, an announcement comes over the loudspeaker that there is an emergency fire drill. What did you tell your students previously to do in this situation?

At the end of the test pick up the papers quickly. It is not fair to let some students work longer than others. If there is a choice always pick up answer sheets first. One word of caution: don't pick up individual tests of early finishers unless they know exactly what they can and cannot do afterwards. Even if you have covered this point, don't leap for the completed tests. You are simply pointing out to others how slow they are.

After the test, try to mark papers within a reasonable amount of time. After all, you are trying to find out what your students have learned. You need that information as the basis of their future learning. Then, too, remember your own resentments when a teacher neglected to give back test papers for weeks afterwards. Your students deserve to know their results. Do return papers and go over the test. If you plan to give it in another year or to another class, collect answer sheets afterwards. You will naturally correct any marking errors you have made. Some teachers require that parents sign a failing test paper, an insurance against future shock at low course grades.

THE STANDARDIZED TEST

Sooner or later you are going to be required to give a standardized test. This can be an achievement or a diagnostic test, but it will always come with a student booklet and a teacher's instruction booklet. Most tests of this kind designed for late elementary and secondary classes also include an answer sheet.

You can prepare yourself for the test by reading the instructions carefully along with a student booklet. There may be mistakes in the instructions or alternatives according to whether an answer sheet is used or not. Pay particular attention to any dictation you have to give. Make sure you are clear on any need for repetition or pronunciation problems.

Check the test to see if any extra paper will be needed. This is true sometimes in certain math tests. Check timing also. If a stopwatch is not available to you, see that you have a watch with a second hand.

During the test check to see that pupils are marking

answers correctly. In this day of machine scoring it is important that marks be made with a soft-lead pencil. They should be dark and fill answer spaces entirely. If a child erases he or she must do so completely and there should be no extraneous marks. In machine scoring it is important not to fold, tear or crumple answer sheets or booklets. Have students handle them carefully.

OTHER EVALUATIONS

Some teachers hate tests. Others love them. If your subject, supervisor, and own personality approve it, you can use other forms of culminating activity besides tests. You will, however, have some objective standards with which to "grade" this activity.

You might use the teacher-student conference. This lends itself well to an area such as beginning language teaching. The purpose of your conference will be to judge students' progress through conversation. You could expect a student to have achieved a specific level of speaking and understanding in order to receive a certain grade. If you have the time and the energy to use the conference as an evaluation tool, you will probably find that it is also valuable in giving you understanding of each individual in your class and the variations of that person's achievement.

A less intimate culminating evaluation is one based on an accumulated mass of student work—the notebook, the journal, the special project, or the folder. Here too you will want to think about your specific standards for grading ahead of time and make them clear to your students. This type of evaluation can be a plus for you by helping you see how each student has developed.

There are other ways to evaluate—the oral report, the practical demonstration of learning, the self-evaluation. They all have the advantage of placing education's emphasis on where it should be: knowledge acquired. They are not used as widely as they might be simply because some teachers and supervisors feel that it is hard to set objective standards. The test will probably always be with us.

EXERCISE

You are teaching a sixth grade unit on consumerism. What evaluations could you devise other than tests to check learning?

SUMMARY

1. All tests should be made to evaluate specific learning.
2. Tests range in length and importance from the quiz to the final exam.
3. Students need to be taught how to take tests.
4. Teachers should prepare themselves to give tests.
5. Teachers should make expectations on test-taking and behavior clear before the test itself.
6. There are other evaluations besides tests.

HOMEWORK

Take the following test. Check your answers with the analysis that follows the test.

Unit Test: Testing

Part One: On the line provided write the letter of the phrase from Col. A that best matches the numbered phrase in Col. B (20 points)

A:	B:	
A. completion test	1. several answers	_____
B. mid-term or final	2. standardized test	_____
C. short-answer test	3. shortest test	_____
D. matching	4. words missing	_____
E. multiple-choice	5. yearly or biannual	_____
F. printed achievement or diagnostic	6. 20 to 50 questions	_____
G. quiz	7. choice between two	_____
H. essay test	8. written paragraphs	_____
I. true-false	9. one sentence	_____
J. unit test	10. corresponding answers	_____

Part Two: Select the best answer and write its letter on the line provided. (20 points)

1. Before a large test you should provide a student with
   A) a pencil B) a quiz C) a review   _____
2. On a quiz you will probably not use
   A) a matching question B) an essay question C) a true-false question   _____
3. In preparing a final exam, the teacher should first decide on
   A) how many points to give B) what type of questions to ask C) what learning to test   _____
4. When a student cheats on a test the teacher should then
   A) decide what to do B) know what to do C) ask what to do   _____
5. During an exam a teacher should always
   A) walk around the room B) stand in the back of the room C) stand in the front of the room   _____
6. A guided composition is writing that
   A) uses numbered lines and special paper B) develops a logical sequence C) answers a logical sequence of questions   _____
7. "Write a 5-sentence paragraph on radiation." These instructions for a 9th grade test are
   A) adequate B) vague C) too specific   _____
8. The conditions in a test room can
   A) be completely controlled B) be planned for carefully C) not affect outcome   _____
9. "Human beings have always been hunting animals," is an example of a true-false question that is
   A) fair B) false C) unfair   _____
10. A non-test evaluation in 6th-grade science could be
    A) collect and orally identify leaves from five deciduous trees B) draw a picture of a deciduous forest C) plant a deciduous sapling on school grounds   _____

Part Three: Complete the following sentences by writing in the missing word. (20 points)

1. Tests measure the _____ as well as the students.
2. Some students with the necessary knowledge may still _____ the test.
3. A _____ should precede all major tests.
4. Test papers should be _____ as soon as possible afterwards.
5. A teacher should always _____ instructions on a standardized test.
6. There will probably be at least _____ parts to a midterm or final.
7. A short test is called a _____.
8. Uniform tests are the _____ for all students of a particular subject level.
9. Standardized tests may either check achievement or be _____.
10. Unit tests should be _____, not dated.

Part Four: Read the paragraph and use its information to select the best answer. Write the letter of the answer on the line provided. (20 points)

Class 102 is taking an end-of-year test in math. Mr. G, the teacher, is watching the class from the back of the room. He notices that Charlie is staring out the window. Charlie is a good student, but he hasn't finished page one yet, and many other students are through. Mr. G begins to collect the answer sheets, but Charlie continues staring out the window. When Mr. G picks up Charlie's paper, there is printed across it in large letters, "I DON'T CARE." These are the only marks on the test paper.

1. This incident in the test period occurs during
   A) the beginning B) the middle C) the end   _____
2. According to the paragraph, Mr. G
   A) has prepared his students for the test B) has not prepared his students for the test C) may or may not have prepared his students for the test.   _____

3. Charlie did not take the test because
   A) he didn't know the answers B) of an undetermined reason C) he didn't care about the test   _____
4. During the test Mr. G
   A) walked around the room B) stood only in the back of the room C) may have been anywhere in the room   _____
5. The students are taking a math
   A) final B) mid-term C)quiz   _____

Part Five: Write a short paragraph (50-150 words) on testing. Answer the following questions: (20 points)

1. What is the purpose of testing?
2. What are some examples of tests and what would each contain?
3. What are some teacher responsibilities before, during and after a test?
4. What are some non-test evaluations a teacher can use?

TEST ANSWERS AND ANALYSIS:

General: Note that the test is divided into five parts of 20 points each. Within each part there are generally ten questions (2 points each) although Part Four has only five questions (4 points each). Throughout the test, because most students are right-handed, answers are marked on the extreme right, except for Part Three. Part Three also could require answers in a separate column to the right, but this may be too difficult for some grade levels. Whenever a test is to be answered in letters, those letters are capitals. It is difficult sometimes to differentiate between a quickly written small *c* and *e*.

Part One: Be careful in this type of questioning to make sure that there can only be one pairing. In this case also Col. A, Letter F gives information that can be used later in the completion section.
1. E 2. F 3. G 4. A 5. B 6. J 7. I 8. H 9. C 10. D

Part Two: Notice that in order to have only one correct answer it is necessary sometimes to have one that is obviously incorrect. Note too that in this section there appear some easy, some average and some difficult questions. In number 9 what was your answer? C and only C is correct because it is far too vague even though it includes that darling of T-F test makers, "always."
1. C   2. B   3. C   4. B   5. A   6. C   7. B   8. B   9. C   10. A

Part Three: Again there are different difficulty levels here. Some of the questions are also double checks of learnings tested in previous parts.
1. teacher; 2. fail; 3. review; 4. marked/graded; 5. preview/pre-read; 6. five; 7. quiz; 8. same; 9. diagnostic; 10. numbered

Part Four: This is typical of reading sections, particularly in non-language arts subjects. You are testing students on reading skills, *not* learnings acquired in the course. These questions take a typical Missouri approach of "Show me." If it isn't in the paragraph, it's not necessarily so.
1. C   2. C   3. B   4. C   5. A

Part Five: This is a guided composition for adults. Each question, therefore, is not capable of being answered in one simple sentence. Most would take several. For younger students questions would be more detailed. You should never ask a question which could be answered with a simple Yes or No.

PART TWO
DEALING WITH STUDENTS

CHAPTER FIVE

HOME SWEET HOMEROOM

THE EXTENDED CLASS

AIMS

1. To understand the scope of nonteaching duties to students.
2. To consider more effective ways of dealing with students on a nonteaching basis.

MOTIVATION

It is Mr. J's prep period, and he is desperately trying to reduce his pile of ungraded tests. Suddenly Kevin arrives, asking for help and obviously upset. Kevin is one of Mr. J's homeroom students. Which takes priority—Kevin or the tests?

**WHAT IS A
HOMEROOM?**

At some point fairly early in life we make an unconscious decision on which is most important to us—people or things. Most of us attracted to teaching opted for people. In the example above, the hypothetical Mr. J. would probably set aside his paperwork to help Kevin. Along with their responsibility for educating students, teachers realize that they have nonteaching duties to pupils also. Nowhere is this more evident than in the homeroom.

The term homeroom is used here because it is universally understood to be a student grouping for nonteaching purposes. In elementary schools without departmentalized teachers the homeroom is simply called the teacher's class. In departmentalized schools it may be called a section or an official class. (Whatever is used in your school should equate with what this chapter calls a homeroom.)

Usually students meet in their homeroom once a day for a short period of time. Aside from the supervision of students during this time, homeroom teachers are generally expected to work on their records, be a contact person for parents, do some rudimentary guidance and perhaps reinforce discipline. Some teachers, particularly in the elementary grades, teach the students of their homeroom, but the particular relationship discussed here is different than that involved in formally educating pupils.

The term homeroom implies a familial relationship between student and teacher. This is very different from the classroom. Some very good classroom teachers are quite poor homeroom ones. The reverse is also true. The skills and organization which support classroom achievement are different than those involved in the personal relationships encouraged by the homeroom grouping. This does not mean that you will be an automatic success in one and failure in the other. This means that you must learn to change gears between teaching and nonteaching situations.

No one has ever seriously suggested that the homeroom teacher be a surrogate parent. Yet many parents and teachers fall into believing this fallacy. Some families find the homeroom teacher the initial contact person. This is the one who may have to call them on absence, lateness, and behavior problems. This is also the one to whom the family may turn when bewildered by John's problems. While you do not have the authority of a parent, you may be expected to act like one—i.e., be interested in all aspects of the student's nonacademic situation.

Some teachers feel that this is an unwarranted responsibility. Perhaps they are right. The fact remains, however, that you may be required by your school or system to have a positive effect on students in a nonteaching situation.

The most likely specific responsibility you will have for your homeroom is in regard to the records of the students. You may have to maintain and update permanent records. You may have to prepare report cards. In doing this you will probably need to write comments, not on student achievement but on student behavior. This is difficult to do if you do not teach your homeroom students. And this probably points up the greatest difficulty in being a homeroom teacher: learning to know your students outside of a teaching situation.

THE HOMEROOM CARD FILE

One way to overcome this difficulty is to set up a card file on each homeroom student with information from the student early in the term.

There are two advantages in having a card file on your homeroom students. First, you have quick access to important information. Second, you can use the card to note the date and briefly comment on any conferences you may have with students and/or parents. It is easy to start a card file. The students can make out the cards according to a form you have set up on the blackboard. It is easy to alphabetize and maintain a card file. It is also a ready source of raw data for comments on permanent records and report cards. There will always be some child in your homeroom who is so quiet that you really cannot know much at all of her or him.

Suppose you are assigned to a homeroom which you do not teach. You want to set up a card file on students, so you hand out cards and show on the blackboard how the cards should be filled out. Notice what questions are asked on the sample homeroom card on page 64.

Suggestion: Learn to consider the parent as neither a friend nor an adversary. You are both adults concerned with a student's progress. At times you may agree, at others disagree. Your job is to be a courteous concerned *teacher.*

Card Form for Homeroom Students

LAST NAME, FIRST NAME   Birthdate

Address

Telephone no.

Mother's full name

Father's full name

How many older brothers/sisters do you have?

How many younger brothers/sisters do you have?

What is your favorite subject?

What is your favorite hobby?

What is your ambition?

THE PARENT-TEACHER CONFERENCE

Mrs. L has written a note asking for a conference with you on her daughter Susan, one of your homeroom students. You know that Susan has been having trouble with her science teacher, and you suspect that this is the reason for Mrs. L's visit. How can you prepare yourself?

The sins of teachers are visited on other teachers. When parents visit the school they may do so as adults, but their attitudes were formed by experiences as students. Those attitudes are bound to affect teacher-parent interviews. Some parents look upon teachers as wise and all-knowing. Others carry resentments from their own schooling. There is only one way to combat this. You must at all times act like an adult and expect the same from parents.

Acting like an adult is not always easy. Sometimes parents are, in teacher terms, unreasonable. You as homeroom teacher, for instance, may be held responsible by parents for problems which have arisen in someone else's classroom. It is difficult to explain in-school procedures to an irate parent. You may be operating on a rational level, but the parent may be on an emotional one. Nothing is accomplished by becoming emotional yourself. Be reasonable, be polite, and if you find that it is impossible to continue, firmly refer the parent to a supervisor.

Don't give up too easily, however. Every teacher at one time or another must deal with an angry parent. If that parent understands you are indeed concerned and want to be helpful, the one-sided battle may become a treaty discussion. You can ordinarily communicate your desire to help with such phrases as, "I understand your concern . . . Let's see what we can do about it . . . Your point of view is helpful." You will immediately turn a parent off with such phrases as, "You must realize that (fill in your own excuse) . . . It's very difficult to (your own excuse)." Educationalese alibis like "We have difficulty remediating his social adjustment to his peers" are just as likely to invoke a resentful parental response. In other words, the more defensive you become the more subjective will be your conference.

Homeroom teachers can become protective of their students, a bad practice when teachers are protecting against parents. You as a homeroom teacher may know of a situation at home of which you disapprove. If it is a crisis problem, it is up to you to refer to a specialist who will help. If it is the more likely noncrisis problem (one child favored over another, a child saddled with too many responsibilities), you cannot as a professional allow your disapproval to color your interview with a parent. First, you know only one side of the story. Second, a student's confidence in your discretion can be shattered by your demonstrating intimate knowledge of the family situation to a parent. It is not easy to rear a son or daughter well. The parent, like you, needs help, and, at the very least, someone open-minded with whom to talk.

GUIDANCE

A teacher is not a guidance counselor. Don't take upon yourself more than you are trained to do.

As a homeroom teacher, you are bound to find yourself at some time in a position where you must advise children non-academically. One of your students is going to ask you a question on values or attitudes. You must answer that question, of course. If you are a sensible, sensitive person, you will answer the question specifically and honestly. But it could be a mistake to think that the question opens an opportunity for you to indulge in some informal counseling unless you are professionally prepared to do it. Professional preparation includes background in getting your own value judgments clear to yourself. You may not be ready for that.

If a student asks you, "What do you think about premarital sex?" it is not an invitation to proselytize. You will, without realizing it, make your attitudes clear to students in the example you set for them. You do not need to bare your innermost thoughts to pupils.

There is also an intrinsic danger for you in your answer to any student question on values. You cannot know what the student will extrapolate from your answer. Teachers have been astonished and embarrassed by fire-breathing parents who have heard the garbled version of a rather mild statement. There are certain households where dinnertime conversation is liberally sprinkled with "But Ms. A says" statements.

This does not mean, of course, that you should never attempt to give students an idea of your own expectations of them. Indeed you can be a powerful force for improvement of student attitudes. As a homeroom teacher you are in a fairly non-threatening position to the student since you will rarely grade on achievement. In a very general way, you can help students be more comfortable and confident in school. You are the one whose smiling "Good morning" or "Look at your new haircut" can send someone off to class in a pleasant frame of mind. Conversely your disapproving "Don't you ever clean your fingernails?" can produce strongly negative results.

You as the homeroom teacher can help students look at their problems and find solutions when the problem is not a deep one. If it is, you are the one who must find help for that student outside of the homeroom.

EXERCISE

Arline has asked to see you after school. At 3 P.M. she begins to talk to you about her boyfriend and suddenly, bursting into tears, says that she thinks she's pregnant. What would you say and do in this situation?

THE INCIDENT BOOK

Conrad, small for his age, is reported to you on March 16 as having cut his physical ed class and gone into the library without a pass. How would you report this as briefly and as objectively as possible?

In the case of a poorly behaved student who belongs to your homeroom, you may be expected to provide anecdotal information to the administration.

The homeroom teacher, like the parent, is the recipient of information that is not always welcome. It is the homeroom teacher to whom the classroom teacher turns many times. Be prepared for the occasional accusatory "Johnny was terrible today" at the time clock. Your responsibilities in terms of disciplining homeroom students can range, depending on custom, from a rather vague duty to admonish in general terms to the specific task of chronicling offenses and reporting them to the appropriate authority.

Here again you are not the parent. The classroom teacher should not hold you responsible for the behavior of children when you are not directly in charge of them. Neither is it your role to defend your homeroom against other teachers. To be effective in your nonteaching relationship with homeroom students, you must remain objective.

One way to do so is through a consistent noting of incidents. You may want to use your cards for this. More likely you will prefer to have a loose-leaf or other notebook arrangement. In this you will have a page for each student. On this you should briefly report the date, place, what occurred and with whom for any student who has behavior problems.

The advantages of such an incident book are several. You may be asked for information about student behavior by the administration. You may want to refer to specifics during a parent conference. You may want to see if a pattern of behavior emerges over a period of time. (Katie and Ms. K. rub each other the wrong way; therefore Katie behaves very differently in Ms. K.'s classroom than in others.) For the administration, for a parent or for yourself, there is an obvious plus in having facts rather than memories available.

GETTING TO KNOW STUDENTS YOU DON'T TEACH

QUESTION OF THE YEAR: How do you get to know your homeroom students well when you do not teach them?

Most teachers are able to assess students and their needs from classroom clues. The homeroom teacher does not have that advantage. If you do not teach your homeroom, you must develop an understanding of your students from being with them for usually brief periods and without the help of revealing classwork, homework or tests. As a matter of fact, your grouping

Tom Jefferson

9/28 Mr. M says threw spitballs at Jane P.

10/4 Custodian found beside broken hall window

10/5 Ms. J says pinched Jane P.

10/12 Aide found in bathroom w/out pass.

10/13 Threw Jane P's books downstairs during dismissal

10/15 Jane P. says kicked her on lunch line

10/20 Observed walking home w/ Jane P.

12/15 Gave Lance bloody nose at recess. Said Lance called Jane P. a monkey.

of students may not exist elsewhere when students have individual schedules. The result of this handicap is that home-room teachers may not get to know their students well. And that's a shame. The teachers who do take the time and trouble to evolve a relationship with their homeroom pupils are capable of having just as profound an influence on them as the classroom teacher. Besides, this is a chance for you to enjoy your students without worrying about having to grade them. But how in the world can you get to know them?

The traditional method is the monitor system. Everyone of us has felt that thrill of pride in being chosen to take the attendance sheet to the office, wash the blackboard, water the plants, clean the erasers, or whatever. The only trouble with this is that unless jobs are rotated someone is always left out. You, as homeroom teacher, will not want to create another in-group. One solution is to work with committees. At the very least it will prepare your students for later life in a bureaucratic society.

Some teachers develop projects with their homerooms. The type of project may reflect anything from a community need to a teacher's pet interest. Usually the latter holds the best chances of a success because it will serve to keep *you* involved and interested, a prime requirement. Particularly with a homeroom that meets only then as a group this type of activity can be good in welding together diverse personalities. The list below may give you some ideas:

Suggested Projects for Homeroom Classes:

1. School improvement
    A. Contributing work
    B. Collecting money
    C. Publicizing need

2. Community improvement
    A. Contributing work
    B. Collecting money
    C. Analyzing and publicizing need

3. Learning improvement
    A. Setting standards
    B. Analyzing needs

4. Group development
   A. Planning and performing a show
   B. Planning and writing a publication
   C. Planning and doing an art project

5. Enjoyment
   A. Planning and going somewhere
   B. Learning a noncurriculum skill or subject
   C. Sharing a noncurriculum experience

Another means of helping your homeroom individuals to become a viable group is to undertake an activity in which there are rivals. You may be competing against the other classes on the same grade level, for instance. Just make sure that your class is as well-prepared for defeat as for success.

If you do want to try a project with your homeroom, set limits well within the children's interest and ability span. If you have a long-range project, it can sag after initial enthusiasm and leave you worse off than before.

Certainly one accepted nonteaching technique to get to know your students is to have a party, particularly to celebrate a holiday. If you do want a party, though, be sure to involve the students in its planning. Even at the earliest ages, students will have more fun and participate more fully when they have suggested what should be done and have helped to do it. You may like the idea of being a Teacher Bountiful, but though it may help your ego it will do nothing for that of your students. Nevertheless, it wouldn't hurt to have the following checklist handy to prompt students:

Teacher's Checklist for Party Planning

   1. When and where will it take place?
   2. Will there be food?
   A. What food will there be?
   B. Who is in charge of bringing/buying it?
   C. How much will it cost?
   D. How will it be paid for?
   E. How will it be served?
   F. Who will clean up afterwards?

3. Will there be music?
   A. Will it disturb other people?
   B. What machine(s) will be needed?
   C. Who will bring tapes/music?
   D. Who will be in charge of choice and volume?

4. Will there be games?
   A. Who will bring the games?
   B. Who will be in charge of participants?
   C. Will there be prizes? Where will they come from?
   D. Who will decide winners?

5. Has the necessary permission been given?

A HOMEROOM IS NOT A HOME

A homeroom is a schoolroom where pupils should feel comfortable. It is not a home, because it must adhere to an educational structure. That structure will be partly dictated by the circumstances of your school. Naturally you will have to take attendance. You may have to distribute notices, letters, report cards, bus passes, lunch passes, or other related papers. You may have other school responsibilities to your students, such as collecting money or assigning lockers.

In addition you will impose your own structure on your homeroom. What that is will be up to you within the restrictions of your school administration. If you are clear within your own mind on your expectations, you should be able to communicate them to your students.

Whatever your attitude may be, though, be realistic. In a home the student is a family member who can reasonably expect some indulgence from others of that small group. In a school the limits of indulgence must be stricter simply because so many people are involved. Twenty-five children cannot all walk around a classroom at the same time. Twenty-five children cannot all have your individual attention at the same time. When a large group is involved, whether you are teaching or not, you must have some rules. You can arrive at those rules on your own or, better still, with your class. As long as they are understood and adhered to by everyone, there should be no resentments.

(One caveat: Students are inclined to be more rigid than teachers in framing behavior standards. Don't be surprised if you have to ameliorate some student-suggested regulations.)

EXERCISE

You have agreed to chair a volunteer group that wants to improve your community. You know no one, and the first meeting is tomorrow. Your problem is twofold. You must see that the meeting accomplishes something, and you must somehow assess what each person can contribute. How would you solve this problem?

SUMMARY

1. Being a homeroom teacher is a nonteaching responsibility.
2. As a homeroom teacher you may keep records, contact parents, facilitate guidance and discipline.
3. An incident book is helpful in discipline.
4. You can get to know your students through observing them as monitors, in projects, and in social situations such as parties.
5. Homeroom should be a structured experience.

HOMEWORK

Seek a group situation in which there are strangers. Observe at least two people for two minutes each. List briefly what you know about them from this observation. Analyze your list to see whether you noticed physical or mental traits. If you noted both, which seemed most important to you? How could you translate this kind of observation to a homeroom?

CHAPTER SIX

MARKS AND SPARKS

CLASSROOM PRACTICES

AIMS

1. To learn classroom routines that save time and tempers.
2. To understand how to best use help in a classroom.
3. To learn how to adapt to various problem situations.

MOTIVATION

Try to remember your "first days" with at least two different teachers. What did they do or say that helped (or confused) you? Why did you have that reaction?

ROUTINES

The classroom is the heart of education. In your many roles as teacher—record-keeper, counselor, peacemaker, example—you are most important to your students in the classroom. It is from that place that your students will emerge with or without some understanding and knowledge of your particular subject area(s). Yet in the classroom, as in so many other aspects of teaching, your effectiveness can be enhanced or decreased by your control of the circumstances surrounding actual learning.

You can make life easier and calmer by setting up for yourself certain routines. These routines will arise in part from your own decision and partly from the administration's requirements. They will always center, however, on particular areas.

ROUTINE #1: SEATING

You are a literature teacher in high school. Some of your work involves students acting out plays in class. In other courses you encourage critical discussion. Given movable desks and an average class size of twenty-eight, could you draw up two different seating plans that you might use?

Older educators remember the rows of fixed desks that no longer impose order on every classroom although they may still exist somewhere. The advent of the movable desk has made life both easier and more difficult for the classroom teacher. It is easier to set up a particular furniture arrangement in the classroom, but it is more difficult to keep that arrangement intact because movable desks are also shove-able. If your students get up and move around during your time with them, any complicated arrangement will go askew by the end of the day. This may not bother you, but you should know that it is possible. In addition, if you share a room with another teacher, discuss any ideas on grouping of desks with that person. Otherwise you may return to a room that is, in your own terms, topsy-turvy.

Movable desks can be set up in a variety of ways, depending on your personal and subject requirements. Some teachers with enough room and a desire to encourage interstudent discussion prefer the semicircle or the U shape. Others who use the small-group or committee technique often will want desk clusters. Teachers who demonstrate or lecture much of the time prefer that all desks face one side of the room. Teachers in shop, art, music, typing or science labs have special requirements that include being able to easily approach each student physically. The diagrams on pages 76–77 may give you seating ideas.

The majority of teachers, when thinking about seating, usually consider the placing of students rather than desks. In large classes there may be an advantage, for instance, in seating students alphabetically by last name. In some situations teachers will seat girl-boy-girl-boy. There may be a reason to seat by height. There is certainly an obligation to seat students with sight or hearing problems as close to the teacher as possible.

Whatever you decide best serves your needs will do so, but

The following diagrams may give you seating ideas:

CLASSIC SEATING PLAN

CLASS _____ PERIOD _____

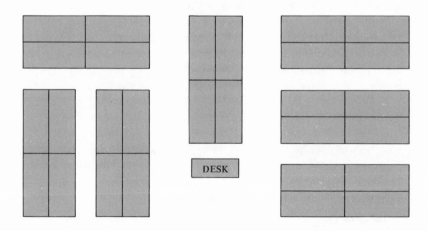

DESK

VARIABLE PLAN

DESK

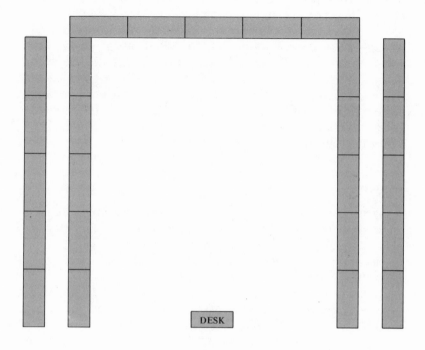

be flexible. You may find that your initial seating plan has flaws. If so, change it immediately. And be ready to change if you observe that certain student combinations lead to problems.

You may prefer a laissez-faire attitude toward seating and let students sit wherever they like. This works as long as you are never absent. You should, though, insist that there be some designation of seating for the substitute teacher who does not know your class. In addition, if students are allowed to change seats frequently, make clear that your rule is first-come first-served. Otherwise precious time is wasted by a late Baby Bear loudly declaiming, "Someone's sitting in my chair."

ROUTINE #2: BOOKS

A teacher overheard: "They put me in that program two weeks after school started. The classes had a substitute who handed out the books. (Pause) And there wasn't one single book receipt." This is accompanied by thunder and lightning sound effects and gasps from the educated audience.

The fact is that books, as objects, can be a headache for the classroom teacher. It is your responsibility to hand them out, keep track of them during the year, and collect them or their monetary equivalent at the end of the year. Students may forget, lose, accidentally or purposely destroy or maim them. Some teachers become so affected by the book syndrome that they refuse to issue texts, using them only in the classroom and sending students home with stacks of purple-printed sheets spilling out of notebooks.

There is nothing wrong with making up your own class-work or homework papers, particularly when a text is not available or appropriate. It is true, though, that we live in a culture which still has a vestigial respect for the printed bound word. Students want textbooks. Parents like to see that children have textbooks. You as a classroom teacher must learn to deal with books.

Your school may have printed receipts for books, like the following illustration, that students make out when they receive their texts. If your school does not, it is a good idea to make up a

Book Receipt

Student: Brian Morrow

Text: American History to 1865

Book #: 56189

Condition: Fair

Date: 9/27/80

LIBRARY BOOKS

Name of Book:	Date Borrowed	Student:	Due:
The House at Pooh Corner	1/15	Tom Tucker	2/1
Street Fair	1/16	Margie Gilligan	2/2
Poppyseed Cakes	1/16	Myra Rosen	2/2

form. At least require a student's signature when the book is issued so there will be no question about its existence.

If you use a text and have issued it, require that students bring the text to class frequently. If you do not, students will have every reason to forget it on the very day when it is essential to classwork. Some students, particularly at the secondary level, have a number of texts, of course, and may have difficulty carrying all of them all the time. You might want to take this into consideration. Make sure, though, that your students understand when they are responsible for having the text available.

Some teachers have books other than texts to issue, in classroom libraries for instance. Set up a sign-out system for these books that is simple but covers the necessary information of student name, date borrowed, book title, and date due. You will probably be able to leave the actual librarian chores to a student monitor above the third-grade level.

ROUTINE #3: HOMEWORK
AND CLASSWORK
RESPONSIBILITIES

The amount of paper generated by one class in a semester can make the routine of handling it a weighty subject. You must develop methods to deal with the twin mountains of homework and classwork.

Be systematic in dealing with homework. If you hand out duplicated or mimeographed assignments, number them. Then follow up the homework. You may want a student monitor to simply check off each person's name, but in addition you have an obligation to do something other than toss that work away. Some teachers grade homework. Some teachers write comments. If you don't feel these practices are appropriate, at least look at what has been done. The purpose of homework is to reinforce what you have taught in class or to pave the way for the new. If you don't look to see what your students have done, you will not know where they are, the bottom line for effective teaching.

You may want to collect homework and keep it in individual student folders to use as the basis of personal interviews. You may want students to keep homework in a particular order in their notebooks or in folders. You may want parents to sign homework, particularly in the lower grades, so that they are aware of their children's progress. Whatever your own choice, don't underrate homework. If you do, how can you expect students to place importance on their outside assignments?

Keeping track of classwork can also be time-consuming. Most teachers find that the easiest way is to require that students keep a notebook or a section of notebook for classwork. Into this will go notes taken by the student, review work given by the teacher, compositions in those classes where there is written work, and other work actually done within class time. If you require your students to do this, check the notebook periodically to see that it is organized as you asked. In addition, you may want to assign a grade to the work at defined intervals.

EXERCISE

Select a subject area with which you are familiar. For a junior high school class in that area, how would you expect a classwork notebook to be organized? What kind of follow-through technique would you use for homework in that class?

ROUTINE #4: OPENING
AND CLOSING PROCEDURES

Think about your most recent experience as teacher or student in a classroom. How did the class begin? Was it effective? Why or why not?

It is easy to drift into bad habits in the way you run your classes. Some teachers, beset with papers and emergencies, never seem to begin a classroom period but rather find themselves suddenly "teaching." Others, especially in secondary schools, lose a sense of time because of their enthusiasm with the lesson and are interrupted in full swing by the change bell day after day. Once in a while there can be reasons for this. If a lack of opening and closing routine is normal, though, the students will probably develop just as casual an attitude toward the class as the teacher.

In beginning a classroom period, a teacher may be required by the school system always to have a Do Now for the students. On the other hand, a written quiz or a quick review may be just as appropriate. Some teachers close the class door as a signal to the class. Some call the roll or check attendance silently, allowing an extra minute for students to settle down. You may simply call a class to order by standing and looking at them.

What you choose to do is never as important as its consistency and its effect on your class. The day has passed when teachers were judged on their ability to Keep a Class Quiet. Some noise may even be necessary for good learning in certain subject areas. But it is true that you must have the students' attention in order to teach them. The only way you know that you have their attention is by requiring it from the beginning of the class activity.

This does not happen automatically. You must train your students through repetition. Let them know what their response should be to your signal, then hold them to it. At first in some classes you may think that you are wasting precious time in waiting for silence. In the long run you will find that this organized approach to learning is welcomed. The day that you don't give that signal, say those words or stand that particular way, there will be students who will ask you, "What happened?"

A closing routine in a classroom is almost as important as an opening routine. In your lesson plan you should have allowed for a summary. Even if you haven't covered what you expected, it is still necessary to briefly restate the learning because it is a reinforcement and focusing of that experience. You may have handed out the homework assignment in the beginning of the class, but you ought always to remind students of it before they leave. In a departmentalized school it is important to get a class out of a room before the next students enter. Make sure to allow for this as much as possible. If someone is in charge of collecting papers, closing windows, or putting chairs on desks, give them time to do this chore.

ROUTINE #5: MARKING

You are teaching a ninth grade algebra class, five days a week. You've observed each student's classroom behavior for an entire semester. There is homework every day. There have been five unit tests. You have given twelve brief quizzes in class. You have also given a midterm. What weight would each of these aspects have in the report card grade? How would you justify that weighting to an administrator or a parent?

There are some teachers whose marking book is a source of never-ending interest to students. They are the teachers who make frequent reference to marks, carry the book around the class often, and have an unnerving habit of peering at a student and then entering *something* in their book. This type of approach places great emphasis on grades as things in themselves. This type of teacher grades homework, classwork, tests, behavior (late arrival, gum chewing), and indeed practically anything.

There are other teachers who appear to ignore grades almost completely except for infrequent tests. Weeks pass before students are aware that they are underachieving in that teacher's eyes. Report card marks come as a complete surprise.

Either of the extremes above is probably resented deeply by students and may present the teachers with problems in giving the final marks. The teacher who marks everything must sift through a large amount of data in order to determine the report card grade. The teacher who marks practically nothing must make a grade decision based on very little information.

In setting up your standards and procedures for marks, try to be as uncomplicated but as fair as possible, as in the example on pages 86-87.

In your marking book you will probably want a section for classroom participation. You may want to give each student a grade for the week, or you may want to note only those students whose participation has been above or below the norm for a particular time period. In your marking book you will also need a section for test results, for projects or term papers, and for homework.

To determine what weight should be given to the various

aspects of student work, you may have to follow school or system policy. If there is none, your subject and grade level will have an effect on the weight of tests in relationship to home- work. At the secondary level, for example, most teachers place more importance on tests than on classwork, except in shop or lab courses.

Whatever your decision on a basis for grades, it is your obligation to communicate that basis to your pupils. If a student knows that the homework will be counted as a third of the grade, that student can gauge its importance more easily. If you accept late work but take points off the normal grade, you should so inform your class long before the work is late. If you have certain standards below which no student should fall, make those standards clear before report card time. And, of course, if the majority of your class is falling below those standards at report card time, it may well be necessary for you to question the norms you have set up.

HELP IN THE CLASSROOM

You are a high school reading teacher with classes in remedial reading. You have just been assigned a Mr. Greco as a paraprofessional in those classes. What will you say after you say "Hello" to him?

Not one teacher in a hundred would admit that she or he could not use help. Yet when it comes to classroom helpers, many teachers ignore the possibilities or even complain of their intrusions. This may be because some teachers feel that the importance of others in the classroom unravels some of the cloak of authority which they feel necessary. More probably it is that teachers simply do not consider the range of possible help they can get.

All of us are used to the monitor system. You can use monitors in the classroom to take attendance, check off home- work, take care of the physical surroundings (windows, plants, blackboards, desks, chairs), keep library or display corners in order, run errands, hand out materials, duplicate information,

Marking

	Homework									
	1	2	3	4	5	6	7	8	9	10
Adams, Jane	✓	a	✓	✓	✓	✓	✓	✓	✓	✓
Anthony, Susan B.	a	✓	✓	✓	✓	✓	✓	✓	✓	a
Curie, Marie	✓	✓	✓	✓	✓	✓	✓	✓	✓	✓
Evans, Mary Ann	✓	✓	✓	✓	✓	✓	✓	✓	✓	✓
Ross, Betsy	✓	✓	✓	a	a	a	a	a	a	✓
Madison, Dolly	✓	✓	✓	✓	✓	✓	✓	✓	✓	✓
Adams, John	✓	✓	✓	✓	✓	✓	a	a	a	a
Carter, Jim	✓	✓	a	a	✓	✓	✓	✓	✓	a
Edison, Thomas	✓	✓	✓	✓	✓	✓	✓	✓	✓	✓
Ford, Henry	✓	✓	✓	✓	✓	✓	✓	✓	✓	✓
Truman, Harry	✓	✓	a	a	✓	✓	✓	✓	a	✓
Washington, George	✓	✓	✓	✓	✓	✓	✓	✓	✓	✓

Book

11	12	13	14	Class Part.					1	2	3	4		Unit 1	Unit 2	
a	✓	✓	✓	+	+	o			90	80	85	60		80	85	
a	✓	✓	✓	o	+	o			75	80	75	75		70	75	
✓	✓	✓	✓	o	o	o			100	100	60	40		90	90	
✓	✓	✓	✓	+	o	+			95	95	90	95		100	90	
✓	✓	✓	✓	o	+	+			100	95	98	100		90	95	
✓	✓	a	a	o	+	o			70	75	60	75		80	65	
✓	✓	✓	✓	o	o	o	+		20	40	35	60		35	65	
✓	a	✓	a	o	o	+	o		65	70	70	85		75	80	
✓	✓	✓	✓	+	+	+	o		100	90	100	80		90	85	
a	✓	✓	✓	+	o	+	o		80	85	85	75		85	85	
✓	a	a	✓	+	+	o	o		90	95	95	90		95	95	
✓	✓	✓	✓	+	+	+	+		100	100	100	100		100	100	

collect money, and a myriad of other tasks according to age level and subject need. Using student labor may sound unfair, but spread over a number of children and a period of time, it becomes extremely useful and is justified in terms of social learning. The key point, of course, is that you will never give all jobs to one or few students. To do so would be a disservice to those students. We have all muttered imprecations against Teacher's Pets in our time.

The monitor is the obvious helper in the classroom. There are more available, though, in most schools. Many school districts employ paraprofessionals, some of whom are more professional than others. You can upgrade the quality of this paraprofessional help in the classroom yourself with a little thought and planning. That thought and planning should be directed to bringing the paraprofessional into the classroom process itself. Most people perform jobs better when they understand the way that job fits into the overall picture. Paraprofessionals are no exception.

You will use the paraprofessional as a record-keeper, of course. But the fact that the paraprofessional is an adult should make the job more than that of a glorified monitor. Even without your experience and training, another adult in the classroom can be a very special ally. You now have two pairs of eyes to see with and two sets of hands with which to help children, and you can be with two groups of children simultaneously.

It is up to you to give the paraprofessional guidance in your viewpoint. Do you want to know which children misunderstood your instructions and need help? When you tell your paraprofessional to walk around and check papers, explain specifically what is to be checked. Do you want to make sure that students are working correctly before those materials are wasted? Ask the paraprofessional to watch for this in one part of the classroom while you take the other. Do you want uninterrupted time with your lowest reading group while the others are doing independent seatwork? Tell your paraprofessional to answer any questions that may arise.

Encourage your paraprofessional to observe children and tell you what is seen. You may not know that Ellie is squirming in a back seat too embarrassed to ask for permission to leave the room. You may be too busy to notice that Eric's nose is touching the paper on which he writes simply because his glasses are in his coat pocket. Those other adult eyes in your room are an invaluable asset.

Paraprofessionals are not teachers although they may be training for the profession. Yet you will want to treat them as teachers in front of the students. They deserve this respect and, as important, are more effective when you make their importance clear to the class. Some paraprofessionals want to and are capable of teaching individuals, small groups, and even entire classes. If it is possible within your system, let them perform in this capacity some of the time. It will not detract from your dominance of the situation. It should give you added insight to your problems and those of the students.

Some systems use volunteers in the classroom, usually mothers. In most respects they can serve in the same way as paraprofessionals although ordinarily on a much-reduced schedule. You should, though, be aware that in a time of emergency or trauma, the volunteer's first instinct will probably be to assume a parental role. In the case of high school or college volunteers, most will be available for only short periods of time and for work with students on a one-to-one basis.

PROBLEMS

The Successful Teacher is an Adaptable Person. As sure as the sun rises in the east, you are going to have problems in the classroom. Some of them, such as behavior, are dealt with elsewhere. Three are mentioned here: overcrowding, small classes and teaching in more than one room.

Overcrowding is a relative term. To the teacher of the 1950s, a class of 45 to 50 students was not particularly rare. In this enlightened era, some systems mandate a class size of 20 to 25. Due to the dropping birthrates, overcrowding is not as common as it used to be. But there are still large classes in some schools, particularly in urban areas.

It is even more important when your class is large that you

have clearly understood routines. In addition you will want to limit movement of students within the room. If possible in your subject area and level, you will want to group students. Even in a so-called homogeneous class you will have underachievers and studyholics. Provide for them in your planning. Do everything you can to streamline paperwork such as test correction. Get to know students better individually by keeping work folders. Watch carefully for any tensions that might arise because of overcrowding and head off potential disruptions before they occur. Talk to a supervisor and see if anything can be done about the class size. Ask for any help you can get in the form of volunteers or paraprofessionals.

Undersized classes present a different problem. Sometimes there are so few students that one can dominate the class discussion. Don't allow this to happen even if the student is brilliant. Encourage everyone to participate, and if the participation is not forthcoming, insist upon it. In a small group also there may be tensions and animosities that would stay below the surface in a large class. Deal with them quickly and firmly; otherwise you will waste time and erode your own control. Be alert to intrastudent relationships. They loom large in a small class.

Time was when teachers were assigned rooms for the entire year and taught in that same space all the time. Now even in elementary school the teacher may travel from room to room. That means you will need to be well-organized in terms of materials. One solution is to leave materials in the various rooms where you teach. If that is not possible, see if there is an office, a book closet or a teacher's restroom nearby which will shelter your things. If there is absolutely no way other than carrying everything with you like the turtle, enlist the help of monitors. Otherwise you will leave school each day with head and shoulders bowed.

SUMMARY

1. Decide what routines you will have and how they will be implemented in seating, books, homework, classwork, beginning and ending a class and marking.

2. Plan to utilize classroom help from monitors, paraprofessionals and volunteers.
3. Be ready to adapt to special problems such as overcrowding, smaller classes and teaching in more than one room.

HOMEWORK

Choose a subject and level with which you are familiar. Make a brief outline of how you will handle specific classroom routines, classroom help, and special problems. Read it through, tear it up, and throw it away. Now write down as much as you really feel you should remember.

CHAPTER SEVEN

BEHAVIOR

SPARING THE ROD WITHOUT SPOILING THE CHILD

AIMS

1. To develop a personal viewpoint of what you will expect in the area of student behavior.
2. To learn how to deal with poor behavior in the classroom.
3. To decide what to do with poor behavior outside of your classroom.

DO NOW

Write a definition of discipline. Write a definition of behavior. Compare and contrast them.

MOTIVATION

Ms. Y is being interviewed for a teaching job in a junior high school. The principal says, "You know, some of our youngsters can be unruly if you let them. What steps would you take in your classroom to ensure good discipline?" What should Ms. Y answer?

BEHAVIOR VS. DISCIPLINE

There is a difference between discipline and behavior although in many schools the words are used interchangeably. Discipline implies that someone has set a fairly rigid standard for the way students should act in a classroom. Behavior, on the other hand, deals with the way students act, both good and bad, aside from any norm. The word behavior was chosen as the subject of this unit because you will be dealing with what actually goes on in your class.

This does not mean that you have no obligation to set standards of behavior for your students. Part of your job as a teacher is to help children learn how to organize the life around them. No one can deal successfully with her or his surroundings without knowing what effect one's behavior can have on that ambience. It is unfair to your students not to define good behavior for them and help them to achieve it.

But what is good behavior? In one class it may mean not chewing gum, not hitting your neighbor, not throwing spitballs, and not speaking without permission. In another it may mean allowing others to take part in class discussion, helping the person beside you, and being responsible for your own litter. To be blunt, in one class the norms are defined in negatives, in the other they are positive. The net result may be the same to a casual observer—two classes working in quiet order. But probably only in the second one will the students feel that they are behaving themselves for goodness's sake rather than the teacher's.

How do you really want your students to behave in class? The current trend in educational books is to deprecate all rigidity in the classroom because, according to the pundits, it will result in either robots or rebels. Not-so-careful readers have made the mistake of substituting the word structure for rigidity though, and feel justified in "letting it all hang out." That "hanging out," unfortunately, can be of a student from a third-floor classroom window, dangerous at the least. You are an adult, your students are not. They will look to you for guidance toward what should and should not be done by them.

You may want to involve your students in setting standards of good behavior. You will probably have more success in making behavior a positive, rather than a negative, when you do involve students. You must first, however, be clear in your own mind on what you expect.

EXERCISE

Use the following checklist to help look at your expectations for classroom behavior honestly:

1. Do I want the class to be silent
   all of the time? some of the time? none of the time?
2. Do I care whether students in my classroom
   eat snacks? chew gum? doodle? look out the window?
3. Does it bother me when students talk to one another?
4. Do I notice when students throw papers on the floor or make some other kind of litter?
5. If a student gets up and walks around the room, do I find it unimportant? distracting? annoying?
6. When a student speaks to me disrespectfully, do I find it hurtful? challenging? unimportant? amusing?

PUNISHMENTS

You are ten years old and fat. Your neighbor in the classroom just remarked on that last fact so you have slapped her. Your teacher is going to punish you. If you could choose, which punishment would you prefer and why?

It is up to the teacher to keep distractions to learning, in this case behavior problems, at a minimum. No human is omniscient, but you as teacher must learn to tune your classroom antenna as sensitively as possible to relationships between yourself and students and between the students themselves. You may be able to prevent incidents by just such sensitivity.

You will, of course, have discussed your expectations on behavior with your class. You should also discuss the consequences that may occur when someone does not come up to those expectations. You will probably have to initiate or monitor those consequences, so make them realistic within your own terms. If you do not believe in corporal punishment even though it may be accepted in your system, don't even suggest that you will use it. If you have no intention of following through on a stated consequence, students will quickly sense this. You will be eroding their confidence in you with possibly serious educational implications.

In the best of all possible worlds every person would be responsible for himself in all ways. There would, of course, be no children in that world. Whether you mean to or not, whether you want to or not, you are at some time or other in your teaching experience going to become an enforcer. Before this happens you should consider what variety is available in terms of castigation other than the physical.

First, there is the talk. This is a teacher-student conference that covers the student's behavior problems and is usually a teacher lecture rather than a two-way conversation. You might keep in mind that the talk is effective only when you know what you expect from the student, have made that clear, and are now asking for an explanation of some variant from this norm. Some teachers use the talk in a subjective way; it helps to ventilate the teacher's resentments about student behavior. Such teachers say things such as, "How could you treat me like that? . . . What have I ever done to you? . . ." This is dangerous psychologically because it implies a deeper relationship between teacher and student than you or your pupil may want to have. You may also find that the talk is more effective when you do let the miscreant speak. Unlikely as it may seem to you at the moment, there may well be a reasonable explanation for misbehavior. We are all entitled to our day in court.

Another of the "mild" punishments a classroom teacher can impose is that of special written work. At first glance this seems excellent, affording a chance to reinforce learning even more. There is, though, one small cloud on the horizon. Could it be that in assigning written work as punishment we are equating the two things? Could it be that we are really teaching students to regard academic work as punishment? Very well, suppose we assign written work totally unrelated to subject learning. Suppose the student copies an admonition or a promise on behavior a certain number of times. By the time the child has written, "I will not throw spitballs in class" 500 times, some teachers think "that'll l'arn him." Unfortunately, children long ago leaped into the era of specialization. Any child with such a task and intelligence will first write "I" 500 times, then "will"—you know the rest. By the time the assignment is completed the student has not necessarily learned not to throw spitballs, just not to be *caught* throwing them if he values his hand muscles.

If assigning written work as a punishment is a mixed blessing, so also is the appeal to parents, supervisors or other teachers. Certainly another person may be helpful in extreme circumstances. But even though that other person may have had more experience than you in dealing with a student's misbehavior, you are bound to lose face with the child when you do not handle your classroom situation yourself. Of course if there is more than one child involved or if the behavior may result in danger to yourself or other children, you must get outside help as quickly as possible.

Some teachers use the grade as a punishment. This may be as formal as a demerit system or as casual as the lowering of a grade for just generally poor behavior. Your decision to use this type of punishment should be governed by two things. First, you should be sure that this option is available to you in your school. Many systems prefer to give a separate behavior grade. Many supervisors do not approve of this mixing of academic and social performance. The second point is that unless you separate the student's academic achievement from behavior, you may penalize the student twice. Some poorly behaved youngsters are also poor achievers.

One final method of castigating students is ridicule. Many teachers use it without realizing what they are doing. It has the virtue of complete immediate effectiveness. In the long run, though, you may have slammed shut any open doors there were between you and the student, not only on a personal but also on an academic level. Ridicule is always unfair, even though your object may seem to be the most obsessive person in the world. Your student is not an adult. You are. You are taking advantage of your superior knowledge and experience to attack someone with unfair weapons. Besides, the street-wise will respond with obscenities, and you can hardly swear back. For the child's and for your own sake, don't resort to teasing or "cute" remarks at someone else's expense. For every student in that classroom you are already the most important person and belittling another won't enhance your position.

While there has been a great deal of publicity in recent years about teaching as a dangerous occupation, it is unlikely that you will be truly menaced by more than a few children in a lifetime of teaching. You will, though, be worn down from time to time by a parade of petty misbehavior and the need to do something about it. It is only natural when there is a large group of people who must remain in close proximity, relatively immobile physically for up to hours at a time, that there should be problems.

WHEN TO REACT

You have been teaching an eighth grade hygiene class for two weeks. Today a student panel is doing a presentation on childhood diseases, so you are sitting at a student's desk in the back of the room. You notice from this vantage point that Demetria Opera is reading something. You reach over, pick it up and discover that she has been looking at an explicit sex magazine. At this moment the class is absorbed in the oral reports. What would you do, and why?

You will find that poor behavior in a classroom ranges all the way from the virtually unpunishable Giggle Epidemic to physical melees. Before you walk into a classroom, you should not only have considered your broad attitudes on why, what and how to set standards of behavior. You must also work out in your own mind the exact point at which you will begin to "notice" poor behavior.

You thought that you should see everything? First, that's impossible even with other adults in the classroom. If you are really intent and involved in the teaching process you (and anyone else) cannot also monitor the movements of every set of hands, feet, knees and lips. Second, there may be times when you don't want to see poor behavior, particularly if the noticing would distract the majority of your students and diminish precious learning minutes. One reason for poor behavior is a desire for attention; your attention could be a reward when you might least want it to be.

How do you know when to pay attention to poorly behaved students? Many teachers use this rule of thumb: *Notice what's happening when it begins to detract from the learning of other students.* This is more or less society's basis for laws, and it generally works in classroom society as well. Of course there are some children who may not be seen by their classmates but are behaving so poorly that you must, in all conscience, do something about it. If you can manage to do that something privately you will probably accomplish more, both with that student and with the class. If you must do something right away (when a child is "taking" someone else's belongings, for instance), stop the student's action but delay exploring the problem till you can do so on an individual basis.

You will find that the same group of students will behave very differently once in a while. If you teach more than one group, that is probably the day when all behave poorly. There is no scientific explanation for this although some teachers fervently believe in air pressure. It is possible that the fault lies in the stars, but it could be we who are the perpetrators. There are days when we feel physically or mentally better than we do on others. If your downs happen to coincide with those of some students, you can walk away from school feeling totally exhausted. When this happens, try teaching something else or in a different way. (See Lesson Plans.) If you can change the physical surroundings by going outside or to the auditorium, do so. Above all, don't get bogged down in an expectation of behavior problems before they occur. It will be a self-fulfilling prophecy.

SHOWDOWN IN ROOM 101

Just as September always follows vacation pleasures, there will come a day when you have a classroom confrontation. You are going to have a student who cannot be corrected gently, indeed refuses to be corrected at all, and either continues inappropriate behavior or defies you verbally. In short, you will be confronting an angry, perhaps verbally abusive child in front of your class. Every teacher has had this experience, and you should prepare for it.

Most of your preparation is mental. You must, in that tense

moment, know that you have done your part to avoid the confrontation. You must be sure that you have been clear on your expectations for the class. Everyone, including newcomers, understands rules and consequences. You must be sure that you are not only fair but appear to be fair, a rather more difficult task.

More of your mental preparation will have dealt with your previous encounters with this student. Has there been any friction before? Was it dealt with to your satisfaction but not the student's? Were there any danger signals—the successively more sullen response, for instance? It is the rare confrontation that descends out of the blue. More likely something has been simmering below the surface for a long time.

If you are clear in your own mind that you have done what you could, not only in general but in specific terms, then you will find the confrontation easier to deal with. There are as many reasons for a child's explosion as there are for an adult's. That child may be under pressures outside of your classroom, pressures about which you can do little if anything. Sometimes the student is overflowing with guilt or inner-directed anger. Sometimes, for no apparent motive, a student will dislike you or will feel that you dislike him or her. None of these emotions can be dealt with easily or quickly in the middle of a classroom period.

When a student attacks or defies you verbally, remember that it is up to you to remain non-emotional. You are the adult, and as an adult you will keep control of the situation only by being objective. You are the person who is old enough and wise enough to know that you may be the surrogate for a parent, a sibling, or even the student's self. Of course, you will not make the mistake of being too wise and too aloof. It is the rare teacher who can successfully smile and shrug off a frontal challenge. But the more low-key your reaction to an angry pupil, the less importance you will give the incident in the eyes of your students.

Most teachers find that an effective way to meet a class-room confrontation is to defuse it, not face it immediately. If you can postpone dealing with the student until the two of you are alone, do so. Suggest that you will see the pupil later or after class. It is important to do this, even though you may appear to be losing ground, i.e., you asked the student to do something, were refused and at least temporarily must accept that refusal. On the other hand, what you asked may have been trivial in comparison with what you could lose by a down-and-out verbal argument in front of the class.

Sometimes a student will simply not stop abusing you. In that case, separate the student from yourself as quickly as possible. Send the pupil to another place, usually a supervisor's office, if necessary with someone else to make sure of arrival. If a student refuses to leave the room, send another student for the appropriate supervisor and request that the child be removed. This is not an admittance of failure on your part as a teacher, or abdication of responsibility, because you will of course discuss the student's behavior on a one-to-one basis as soon as possible.

Do not discuss the incident with the rest of the class. It is your job to let such distractions take as little time and effort away from your teaching as possible. Pick up the threads of your lesson immediately and plunge ahead as if nothing happened. Your calmness in this will be another indication to the class of your control.

After an incident, write a brief paragraph describing what occurred with actual quotes and no editorializing. It is quite likely that a parent will be involved, and it helps in later discussions to deal with as many facts and as little emotion as you can. Of course you are going to get angry somewhere along the line, but keep the demonstration of that anger to a minimum before class, student, and parent. Do explode and get it out of your system, but only with family and friends.

EXERCISE

The meaning of the following note was clear to the dean of discipline but it needed rephrasing before being entered on the student's file. How could it be worded more factually? "I have had it! This is the umpteenth time Lily has cleaned her purse in Lit. Her chair is surrounded by scraps of paper and, as she loudly pointed out, the holder of her birth control pills. Do something! Please!"

GETTING HELP

In many schools, classroom behavior is not only the concern of the teacher but also of a supervisor. Some supervisors are designated disciplinarians, others include the job with their other tasks. In addition there are schools, particularly at the secondary level, which have a dean or deans of discipline. When and how do you involve these people in your problems with misbehaving students?

If your school is large, there is probably some sort of printed guide for you on what behavior referrals should be made and to whom. Ask for it and study it. In this and in schools which do not have so formalized an approach, you will probably find that the classroom teacher is responsible for day-to-day behavior standards, and out-of-class personnel handle the unusual and/or dangerous situations.

In the eyes of supervisors, teachers generally make one of two errors in deciding whether to refer students for outside discipline. First, there is the teacher who prefers to handle all problems within the classroom, even when there is a physical fight. This can be both dangerous and not good sense. If the student is involved with other teachers and problems that stem from out-of-school reasons, you alone cannot "solve" the situation. As a matter of fact, there may not be a solution within that particular school. Another mistake made frequently is to refer all misbehavior cases for outside disciplining. This should not be necessary and may perhaps be detrimental to your relationship with a class who would see you as incapable of handling routine misbehavior.

When a youngster is referred to personnel outside the classroom, be sure to write any pertinent information about the behavior incident on an $8\frac{1}{2}$ by 11 paper (unless there is a particular school form) with the date, time, or period in which it occurred, and sign it. Write details and facts without subjective conclusions. Others can deal far better with "Refused to change seat. Said, 'I hate you and this course.' " than "Behaved toward me with disrespect."

Sometimes, especially in the case of the chronic misbehavior problem, you may be asked to contribute something to a student's case history. Here again, concentrate on the facts. "Dennis is a mountain of silence" may read poetically but is not likely to appeal to social workers or psychologists.

DEALING WITH MISBEHAVIOR
OUTSIDE THE CLASSROOM

One of the knottiest answers to unravel is to the question, "What should I do about behavior outside of my classroom?" There are almost as many possible replies as there are teachers. Most of them conclude "Something" or "Nothing."

The decision may not be yours to make, of course. There may be clear guidelines in your school on student behavior in halls, stairwells, cafeteria, auditorium, and entryways. Most of the time, though, you will probably have to choose the attitude that you will take when that behavior is not acceptable.

Some teachers believe that their responsibility for student behavior extends beyond the classroom walls only when their class is being led to or from the classroom or is in an assembly. They feel that it is up to supervisors and other personnel to deal with misbehavior elsewhere in the school. This is even the tradition in some schools.

Other teachers are ready to rush in where principals fear to tread. They separate students fighting in the street and may even point out faults to strange children in busses and elevators. If you are ready to take the responsibility for pupil behavior, you cannot slough it off at the school door, say these teachers.

Probably most teachers follow a middle path. If there is poor behavior or a dangerous situation within school grounds, they will most likely become involved. At the very least they will report the incident to someone who can deal with it. If something occurs beyond school grounds that seems to bear on previous incidents, teachers may feel constrained to refer the matter to an appropriate person but not become physically or verbally involved.

There are some times, such as cafeteria duty, when the teacher's responsibility for guiding student behavior is clear. If you do have out-of-classroom duty, you will want to be sure that you know the school's policies on behavior. What you do within your classroom may be different than what you are allowed to do elsewhere in the building or playground.

SUMMARY

1. Since you are responsible for your students' classroom behavior you should understand that it will be based on expectations that you have developed and made clear to them.
2. In dealing with poor behavior, make the consequences of it clear beforehand to students and follow through when necessary.
3. In a confrontation with a student, keep cool and defuse the situation by delay if possible. Where not possible, separate the student from the class quickly.
4. Limit requests to out-of-classroom personnel for aid in behavior problems to dangerous or extreme misbehavior. Be clear in referrals on the facts of poor behavior.
5. Decide what type of responsibility you will take for out-of-classroom behavior before the need arises.

HOMEWORK

Read the following short history and decide at what points and in what ways you might have handled the situation differently. What do you think will happen here?

Ms. R is teaching Level I Spanish to a tenth grade class. The students are in the middle of a class quiz on the preterite form of regular verbs. Questions are on the board, and everyone is writing the answers. Everyone except Glenn. As Ms. R walks around the room to see how everyone is doing, she sees that Glenn's paper is blank and he is busily carving a word on the side of his desk.

"Stop it, Glenn, " says Ms. R. He smiles at her and replies, "How are you going to make me, Teach?" and continues his handiwork. "You're defacing school property," protests Ms. R. "Who cares?" he shrugs. Other students have begun to notice the exchange. Ms. R sees heads turning. "Continue your work, class," she admonishes. "It's just Glenn doing some interior decorating he shouldn't."

For some reason this remark seems to sting Glenn to the quick. He leaps to his feet, shouting, "I ain't no interior decorator. I'm a man." Bewildered, Ms. R backs away from Glenn's carelessly held penknife. "Sit down," she orders, "and be quiet." "No," says Glenn, "I'm not sitting down till you apologize for calling me that."

By this time all the students have abandoned their quiz. Rosemarie offers, "I'll go get Mr. Scarlatti, Ms. R." "That won't be necessary," snaps the teacher. "I can take care of this. Give me that knife, Glenn." She moves closer to take the knife. Glenn backs away, but in doing so, he trips and somehow slashes her palm. Both he and Ms. R stare in shocked silence at the red line of blood on her hand.

CHAPTER EIGHT

CLASS WITHOUT WALLS

HOLD HANDS, CHILDREN, AND HAVE FUN

AIMS

1. To learn how to pre-plan, organize, and take a class trip.
2. To understand how community resources can be better utilized by and for students.

MOTIVATION

In the year 2041, Eloise's cousin Frank is visiting her from out of town. After exchanging family news, he says, "Listen, you can do me a big favor. Take me to see the hydroponds. I hear they're fantastic." She stares at him in surprise. "Who would ever want to go there?" she asks. "Everyone knows what hydroponds look like." Frank subsides into sulky silence.

WHERE AND WHY

A cliché in New York City is that no native New Yorker ever visits the Empire State Building. Activities like that are left to the tourists. This slightly superior attitude is often reflected in a teacher's approach to a class trip. Certain destinations are discarded because they seem so obvious. The reverse is also true. Some classroom teachers believe that any excursion beyond school walls is beneficial to the students whether it has bearing on their learning needs or not.

Neither attitude is particularly defensible. A class trip may have many purposes, but its main aim must be educational. Just because students have visited a museum with their parents does not exclude it from a visit with you for specific learning reasons. Conversely, just because the circus is fun does not make it a valid place for a class trip unless there is an educational point. Your lesson plan begins with the aim, and the true beginning of any class excursion should be the educational purpose for it.

This does not mean that class trips cannot be enjoyable. One of the pleasures for you and your students will be the chance to see one another in very different circumstances, unobscured by all the paraphernalia of the classroom. While you and the students are always engaged in a joint venture, the class trip serves to point up this sharing of experiences. If you are able to handle the excursion unobtrusively and well, you will probably be reaping human-relations dividends for weeks afterwards.

The educational purpose of a trip should be easily explained and understood by parents, supervisors and students. The easiest type of trip is the trip related to current classwork. This is the excursion whose purpose is to show concrete examples of classroom abstractions: the rock-hunting expedition in a local park or the biology displays at a natural history museum, the play performance of something read in class or the assembly-line tour of a raw-to-finished product studied. Given a large enough community, you should be able to develop several possible trips with such obvious purposes.

Another type of class trip is not as closely related to current learnings, but is also educationally valid. This is the trip designed to initiate learning, usually of a process. For example, you might organize an excursion to a local newspaper for a class planning to make its own publication. You might plan the observation of a television production for a group that will be videotaping its own program. Here again, the educational purpose is made clear quickly to everyone involved.

Finally, there is the class trip whose educational purpose may deal with affecting student behavior. This is the Spanish class visit to a Latin-American neighborhood or restaurant, or the student-performed program at a local hospital or retirement home. The educational purpose of this type of trip is usually not closely related to specific current or future classroom learning. Yet it may have an obvious tie to a valid educational aim of cultural understanding or societal responsibility.

EXERCISE

Select a subject area and grade level with which you are familiar. Using your own community, develop educational aims for three possible class trips, one for each type mentioned above: current learning, initiating learning, and affecting student behavior.

STUDENT INVOLVEMENT
IN TRIP PLANNING

Once you are clear on the educational aim and the destination of a class trip, you must plan its organization. In doing so, according to the age of the students, you may want to involve them. Whether or not they help, however, there will be four basic phases of your organizing.

First, you (and perhaps the students) will want to work out the details of the trip, the when, where and how of it. You may find it necessary to go through the physical part of the trip yourself ahead of time. This becomes particularly important with a large group or younger students. Taking the trip yourself beforehand gives you an opportunity to consider such factors as the way you pay admissions, location of rest rooms, and facilities for eating. Making the excursion yourself can also give you a better idea of the time involved in transportation and in the visit proper. If you are unable to preview the trip in person, perhaps you can get the pertinent information from someone else—another teacher or someone at the facility you will be visiting.

The next step in organizing the trip will be for you to prepare the class. Students should know why they are making the excursion and what they are expected to do or see on it. If the trip is aimed at making current learning more real, you should encourage pupils to discuss what their expectations are. If the trip is to initiate future learning, children should know that they will be expected to use the acquired knowledge in a later activity. If there is a cultural or social purpose for the excursion, the class should be able to analyze its value for them ahead of time.

In addition to preparing students academically for the trip, you should also have them consider what behavior is appropriate outside of school. Behavior in this case should include more than a vague view of comportment. You should discuss with your students where and how they should form groups for nose-counting, what to do if someone is lost or left behind, where and how lunch will be bought and/or eaten, and other specifics. Even at the most advanced secondary school level, you will be responsible for your group's physical safety and well-being. This will be easiest when you and your students know and follow a plan.

Finally, in organizing a class trip, try to include other adults. For your own protection you will ask parents to sign permission forms. In addition, you may want to invite them to accompany you. If you have been working with paraprofessionals or volunteers, you will want to invite them also. And some teachers find it easier to make a trip jointly with another teacher and class.

EXERCISE

Take one phase of organizing a trip: planning physical details, preparing students academically, preparing students in behavior, or including other adults. Work out a checklist for yourself on this one phase. Compare it with the following:

Preplanning Checklist
for Class Trips

Physical Details:
1. Must you make reservations?
2. Is there an admissions charge?
3. If there is an admissions charge, will the school pay or must you collect it from the children?
4. Are there any special hours when large groups must visit?

5. What and where are the facilities for:
   a. eating
   b. restrooms
   c. souvenirs?
6. Is there any special kind of dress required?
7. Are there guides, and if so, should they be paid or tipped?

Transportation:
1. Which form of transportation is easiest, quickest, cheapest?
2. Who pays for transportation?
3. If a school bus is needed, how is it reserved? Are there any restrictions on time?
4. If commercial transportation is used, must the driver be paid or tipped? Do you need cash or a check?

Approval:
1. Must this trip be approved by a supervisor? If there are school forms for approval, how far in advance must they be filled out?
2. Are there parental forms in the school or should you make your own?
3. Are there any special restrictions of which you should make supervisors or parents aware? (dress, special hours)

Preparing Students Academically:
1. Have you explained the educational purpose of the trip clearly to the students?
2. Should students prepare a list of questions to ask or information to find?
3. Have students discussed their expectations in class?
4. Are students clear on what type of follow-through you will require from them after the trip?

Preparing Students in Behavior:
1. Do students understand what they should and should not bring on the trip?
2. Do students know what type of dress is appropriate for your destination?

3. Do students know when parental permission and money is due?
4. Do students know how and when they should line up, if at all?
5. Do students understand whether and how much money they should bring?
6. Have you discussed lunchroom and restroom provisions with the class?
7. Do students know what to do if they become lost/ill/injured?

Including Other Adults:
1. Have all adults who work with students been invited to accompany you?
2. Have parents been invited to accompany you?
3. If other adults are going on the trip, have you discussed what help they may give you?
4. Are there provisions in seating/eating/admissions for the adults accompanying you?
5. Are the other adults aware of the educational purpose of the trip, and how they can help you achieve it?

THE TRIP AND AFTER

At last the day of the trip arrives. So does the lone child who still has not turned in signed permission, and that child is still sans form. What should you do? Strictly speaking the only thing is to arrange that the child spend the day with another class in school. On the other hand, there may be a perfectly valid reason for the form's not arriving in your hands, even though the parent has given permission. If you feel that this is true, with your supervisor's approval you might call the parent and get oral permission on the phone. But be aware that this is risky. In many states when an untoward accident occurs, even though it may be unconnected with your own negligence, the school can be sued for damages. Any proof you may have, to show that parents were aware of and permitted your trip, can help under those circumstances.

You're off! Ah, what a relief it is. Here is the whole outside world, scurrying about its adult business. How bright everything is. This is almost like a vacation, isn't it?

No. It isn't. You are as much on the job traveling with your class as you would be in a classroom. While you may be feeling akin to the other adults you see, in their eyes and your students' you are still the teacher. As the teacher, you must be ready for everything that comes. A class trip is not a time for you to relax, so don't expect it.

Is there a jammed candy machine? Guess who's in charge of unjamming it. Is someone's finger stuck in the top of a soda bottle? Guess who looks for the soap. Who patches knees, dispenses Kleenex, finds lost souvenirs and lends a shoulder for the exhausted tourist? You know who. The problems may be different, but the situation is the same. On a trip, as in a classroom, you are in charge of solving most problems. Even if there are other adults on the trip with you, you are still the final authority.

Once a trip has been taken, you are also in charge of its evaluation. There are really two levels to this evaluation. You will, of course, sit down by yourself and think through the excursion to see what went well and what didn't. You may want to put these thoughts down on paper for future reference. This postevaluation can be of help not only if you plan to go to the same destination again, but it can also aid in planning trips to other places.

You will certainly want to have your students evaluate the trip as well. There will be classwork based on the trip, but besides that you will want to know exactly what was good and not-so-good in the students' eyes. You may be surprised to hear of the impression a relatively minor factor may have had. Don't get discouraged when you find that Johnny thought the best part of *H.M.S. Pinafore* was when they came down the aisle selling popcorn at intermission. At least the experience was positive, and next time he may even begin enjoying Gilbert and Sullivan.

Even when a class trip has flopped in your eyes—it rained, everything was closed, you were late, someone was lost/nauseated/hysterical/faint—your students and you have probably learned something. As Lamar said thoughtfully, "I learned that I do not like hot dogs with sauerkraut." Negative learning can be important, too.

Checklist for
Evaluating Class Trip

Physical Details:
1. Was it appropriate in size, orientation, expense and interest level for your students?
2. Were there any unforeseen complications with
   a. lunch
   b. restrooms
   c. cost?
3. Was the visit at an appropriate time of the day or year?

Transportation:
1. Was it adequate in space, length of ride and cost?
2. Were there any unforeseen expenses or dangers for the students?

Approval:
1. Did you neglect to notify someone who should have known about the trip?

Academic Preparation:
1. Did students understand the process demonstrated or gain the knowledge that you hoped?
2. Are students able to see the connection between their trip and what you are teaching them in the classroom?
3. Was the follow-through you planned appropriate for the actual trip experience?

Behavior Preparation:
1. What went wrong and why?
2. Were students cooperative in lining up or being counted?

3. Did students know how to behave
    a. at your destination
    b. on transportation
    c. at lunch
    d. in restrooms?
4. Was there any incident for whose occurrence you might have prepared the students?

Other Adults:
1. Did they help? If not, why do you think they did not?
2. Was any of their behavior inappropriate? If so, what can you do about that next time?

THE WORLD INSIDE

The trite vision of a school as separate from the world has hopefully passed into legend. Some relating of learning to the community comes from taking students on class trips. But this is not the only way in which to open classroom walls. There are at least two more.

One involves bringing the community into the classroom itself. This is done somewhat by the use of paraprofessionals and volunteers. It can also be accomplished on a one-time or short-term basis by the use of parents, other speakers, and films or programs.

Parents are a resource that teachers tap frequently for moral support. But they can be more. Parents are adults, many of whom have interesting skills or knowledge to impart to youngsters outside the home. (And for parents read guardians and other relatives.) Rajeh's grandmother is visiting from India where she is supervisor of a large city's schools. Her visit to school can be an important event in the social studies class. Olympia's father has just finished illustrating a book. His detailed presentation of the work and how he does it opens vistas in a career guidance class. Housekeepers, for example, have many skills to be demonstrated from babytending to gardening. You can find out which people are available with a formal questionnaire or informally by listening to student conversation clues. You can also do it by being alert to possibilities from those clues. There may well be a classroom application for Ms. L's childhood collection of post cards. It is up to you to draw that conclusion.

There are other classroom visitors available to you besides the parents. The butcher, the baker, and candlestick maker are all people who lead lives that can prove valuable to your class. Government institutions, from the fire department to the department of health, are a likely source. Even those of us who are ordinarily inarticulate can usually summon up enough poise to speak on a topic in which we are interested and knowledgeable.

If you cannot round up live people from the community to speak or demonstrate in your classroom, you can probably get hold of special films or programs. Some large organizations, such as the telephone company, welcome the chance to be called upon. It is good public relations. Some small organizations such as local dance or theater companies also welcome the chance to perform. Experience is valuable to them. You will, of course, preview any film before you show it to a class to make sure that it is accurate. You will, naturally, also see the program you might want to present in school to verify its appropriateness for your group.

In order to find either speakers or programs for your classroom, you will have to use ingenuity. If you are a local resident, use your eyes and ears to spot someone of interest during your shopping. If you want to draw on business resources, call the chamber of commerce. Or take courage in hand and phone a large company yourself. Ask for the person in charge of public relations, and chances are the response will be encouraging.

Anything which you as a teacher can do to show students that what is learned inside school walls has a strong relationship to what is needed outside the school building, has to be a plus. You may want to check with your supervisor when you are planning for a visitor, and invite that supervisor and other teachers to the room for this special event. Contrary to what you might believe, the presence of other adults will probably be encouraging to an outsider. Most non-educators find groups of students far more intimidating than adults.

EXERCISE

Think in terms of your own community. Then, using a familiar subject and grade level, make a list of possible sources for outside speakers. Use the following to help you.

Possible Sources for Outside Speakers in Your Classroom

Parents or Relatives:
1. Has someone taken a long trip recently?
2. Has someone an unusual hobby or occupation?
3. Has someone a collection tied in with class activities?
4. Has someone a special ability that can be demonstrated?
5. Has someone artifacts from the past or from far away?

Other Speakers:
1. Producer or vendor of something studied in class
2. Representative of the fire department, the police department, the health department, sanitation, housing, welfare, hospitals, colleges or universities, government, media, transportation
3. Representative of community groups: parents, environmentalists, businesspersons, occupations, professional organizations
4. Representative of large company or industry: telephone, other utilities, manufacturers, services, government services

Films and/or Programs
1. National or regional companies, trade associations, service organizations, governmental departments
2. Local community drama, dance, theater groups, radio/TV stations, local theater owners/managers
3. State/municipal government, colleges/universities, state departments of education, federal government agencies

THE WORLD OUTSIDE

The third way to relate learning to life directly and easily is to take the class into the community, not simply on a visiting basis, but with the purpose of becoming involved.

The obvious example of this is the social studies class carrying on an in-depth exploration of a local governmental organization. This is different from a trip which may be observation of a court session, a visit to town hall, or a tour of the police station, because it involves students more deeply with what is going on in government. Some secondary schools arrange exploratory apprenticeships with those in office. Some small towns have a day when local students take on specific governmental jobs. Where students feel strongly about a particular issue, they may be involved in presenting petitions or oral arguments. These activities usually make a profound impression on students, but be careful before you become too enthusiastic about this approach. Be sure that anything you do in terms of student impact on government is well-planned, supported by your supervisor and your parents, and, most of all, something which has meaning to the class.

A class can also become a part of community activity by planning a way to have a positive effect on it. Such a class might carry out an environmental change—cleaning a vacant lot, painting murals on blank-walled buildings, or planting trees. Groups of students who are interested in changing attitudes might visit homes to tell consumers of their rights or help store owners clean sidewalks to offset low public opinion of students' social behavior. Here again you must pre-plan carefully and make sure that what your class is doing can be justified educationally.

One way to involve learning with life is to have students visit other schools and contribute in some way to the learning there. Your children can be tutors, demonstrators, or reporters. They can help younger students or be helped by older ones. They can find out what the next level school will be like or interpret their own experiences for students at a lower grade level. To arrange this sort of experience for your class, you must be clear on what the students plan to do and make sure this is acceptable to supervisors and teachers in the other school as well as your own.

Finally, students can be of help in local institutions such as hospitals or rest homes. They can give programs, write letters, read aloud, or physically help patients. Be sure that any such activity is approved by both your school and the student's family. While its philanthropic value is obvious, there may be objections of which you are not aware. And above all, have an educational purpose for this activity, otherwise you are serving once again to isolate "real" life from school learning, the opposite of what you may desire.

SUMMARY

I. The stages of a class trip are

  A. Planning the educational purpose and selecting the site
  B. Pre-organizing through
    1. Familiarity with physical details
    2. Helping students be aware of the academic reasons
    3. Preparing students on behavior and procedures
    4. Including other adults who can help
  C. Evaluation afterwards by yourself and by students

II. Community can enter the classroom through the use of parents, outside speakers, films and programs.

III. Students can go into the community to apply learning through impact on government, changing physical conditions or attitudes, entering other schools or institutions.

HOMEWORK

Read the following account of a class trip by a student. Find and list the points at which, as the teacher, you might have done something differently.

Yesterday we went to the planetarium with Ms. Haydock. It was fun, but not like I expected. Ms. Haydock said I couldn't take my camera because it might get lost or stolen, so I had to leave it in Mr. O's office. Then when we got on the bus she was real crabby. Some of the kids were sitting three in a seat, and she yelled at them. Jackie King stood up when we went around a corner, and he fell down and split his lip. The bus driver had a First Aid Kit, but Ms. Haydock was yelling like crazy.

When we got to the planetarium we were too early for the

show, so they wouldn't let us in. We were going to eat lunch afterwards but Ms. Haydock said we should do it Now, so we went over to the park and started eating. I didn't want my sandwich so I started feeding it to the pigeons. Ms. Haydock came over and started shaking my arm and saying Don't be a Litterbug. When I tried to explain to her it was for the pigeons she just shook my arm some more.

Finally we went inside the planetarium and saw the show. It was sort of dumb. I didn't understand what they were talking about half the time. We never had that in Science class. The best part was when the lights went out, and I pinched Susie. She started crying and Ms. Haydock had to take her outside, so then we got to sit by ourselves and go "Oooh" and whistle at the shooting stars. I saw one of the guards talking to Ms. Haydock later, and she looked like she wanted to cry.

When we got back on the bus, Mike Caputo was missing. Ms. Haydock sent Buba to look for him, but then Mike came back and Buba was lost. Finally everyone was on the bus, and we drove back to school. We were so late I couldn't get my camera back, and my dad was so angry he shouted that he's going to school and tell that dumb teacher What for.

I think the best part of the trip was when Jackie split his lip. I never saw so much blood in all my life before.

CHAPTER NINE

AUDIO-VISUAL ENVIRONMENTS AND MACHINES

HOW TO GIVE A CLASS ROOM

AIMS

1. To learn how to use the physical environment of a classroom effectively.
2. To understand various uses of machines to enhance learning.

MOTIVATION

Ms. F's classroom is a model of roomkeeping. Her window shades are even, blackboards are clean, and students scrub the desks before every holiday. In contrast Mr. L's room is cluttered with animal cages, student projects, and plants. Yet somehow students are always making excuses to visit Mr. L. They seem to find his mess interesting.

HOW TO TEACH SILENTLY

American families pay millions of dollars each year to interior decorators to design rooms in their homes. American companies pay billions of dollars each year for professional decoration of everything from factories to executive washrooms. Schools, on the other hand, where most people spend a great deal of time between age 6 and 18, are dependent for decor on very little money and lots of ingenuity from teachers. And the physical environment of a classroom can help open or close minds to learning.

There is not much you can do about the basic form of your classroom. There is plenty that can be accomplished, though, within the limitations of the usual blackboarded, bulletin-boarded, window-and-walled rectangle in which you and your students live for the better part of the year. And it is important to do something. If you want students to believe that what you are teaching is important and interesting, you must say this to them in many different ways. Your room should say it also.

The first thing to do is to survey what your room is like physically. Are the windows susceptible of decoration or would that interfere with their opening and closing? Are there window-sills on which you can place things? What possibilities are there in terms of bookcases—if they're low ones can you utilize their tops? Can cabinets be left open for special displays? How many bulletin boards are there? If there is a lot of wall space are there any restrictions made by the school on how you cover them—for example, the use of sticky tape? Are the ceilings high enough so that you can hang things from them? If you have money and energy to devote to painting walls, will the administration or the custodian object?

Sometimes it is helpful to note what your colleagues have done with their rooms. While you will not want to imitate anyone, there is value in seeing what the range of possibilities is within your school. At the least, you will learn what you don't want to do.

In addition, you will want to explore inexpensive or free sources of room-decorators. Suggestions here deal with plants, posters, student work, art projects, and teacher-made displays. You are not confined to these by any means. Check your local community for any unusual sources of help in decorating. Look at your own home to see what you can glean from your personal experience in decor.

Plants are a standby in decoration. Clippings started in water can be enormous in a very short time. As a matter of fact, some plants can be grown totally in water. Most classrooms have a great deal of light, the prime requisite for successful indoor gardening. And the plants themselves can be educational, particularly if you branch out into such things as vegetables and herbs. If your windowsill is not wide enough, plants can be hung from the ceiling or grouped together on a nearby bookcase or empty desk. Containers do not have to be ordinary plant pots. If the school has a ceramics shop, you may have a ready source of unusual holders. There is, as a rule, only one real drawback in using plants for classroom decoration. That is the June day when you stagger home with your arms full of greenery. It seems a small price to pay, though, for something so inexpensive and attractive.

Another inexpensive, attractive source of decoration is the poster, or similar large picture. Travel agencies, travel bureaus, consulates, and offices of foreign countries are a good source of free posters. There are other less obvious possibilities, too. Some calendars, even if outdated, have attractive large pictures which can be cut away from the other material. Some large companies often put together a poster series for a specific purpose such as factory safety. Some movie/theater groups have extras of large advertisements. There are government posters available from various offices or departments, including your own and other state travel promotion departments. Some national organizations have posters available. Some magazines (other than *Playboy)* have fold-out pictures, charts or maps. Check a local book store to see if part of the book advertising that the owner receives could be appropriate for your room.

The one thing to remember, of course, with any material from a commercial source, is that you are under no obligation to be an advertising medium. Have no hesitation in clipping off any advertising material from posters. Its place is not the classroom. On the other hand, promotional material for geographical locations is usually considered unobjectionable.

Another ready source of interesting wall-covering is student classwork, tests, or homework. This is interesting not only to the students who have produced the work but also to visiting parents. There are one or two caveats, however. First, be sure that the work is well done. It is embarrassing to a teacher when obvious mistakes have not been corrected and are discerned by a visitor, aside from the poor example it sets for students. Second, be sure to keep this type of work current. Yellowed essays on a topic that the class studied months ago have outlived their usefulness and show you as less involved than you may be.

Other student work can make an interesting display. Student-drawn maps or charts can be colorful. Pictures, mobiles, and dioramas may also be available. Student art projects, even if they result from a class other than your own, such as industrial arts, are another source of decoration. Sometimes students can be prevailed upon to bring in their collections—rocks, stamps, match covers, postcards, and what-have-you—are all possibilities.

The final inexpensive resource you have is your own ingenuity. The school usually has large colored paper available. Even if you do not consider yourself artistic, you should be able to do certain things. With colored paper you can create collages from magazine pictures, reproduce apt quotes in large print, make lists centered around some aspect of your subject—let your mind range. You might have one section of your bulletin board for a trivia quiz (answers printed upside down), for a historical gossip column, or for a did-you-know question of the week.

In whatever way you choose to furnish your room, do keep in mind that the purpose of the activity is to teach students something about your subject area as well as to make a more pleasant atmosphere. A social studies teacher who displays reproductions of famous art without pointing up their relationship to that subject area is missing a good teaching bet.

DECORATING THEMES

Sometimes you may have decorated your room very carefully in the fall for a Parents' Night and then gone on to other things. Suddenly a stray sunbeam reveals that everything has become dusty, bedraggled and—let's face it—old. You really can think of nothing in particular that you want to do, but you know that you must change something. Here are a few suggestions that may help.

Perhaps you can do something with the season. Even high school students respond with delight to something colorful taped on the windows. You can make snowflakes out of plain typing paper folded into fourths, then thirds slantwise, and clipped in various ways. You can make Christmas trees out of green paper folded in half, traced and cut out. Tulips are easily cut from red or yellow paper with a straight thin piece of green as the stem.

Sometimes holidays are a theme for decoration. Everyone is familiar with Hallowe'en, Christmas, Easter and Independence Day. But there are other less well-known events. National Book Week is the third week in November. January was the birth month of a number of American patriots—Paul Revere, Betsy Ross, Alexander Hamilton, Benjamin Franklin, Robert E. Lee, and Franklin D. Roosevelt. The third week in March is Hobby Week, the last one Health Week. Shakespeare was born in April. So was Joseph Pulitzer, founder of the prize named after him. May 18 is Peace Day, World Good Will Day. The Magna Carta was signed in June. See the table on pages 128–131 for more ideas.

Another way to quickly change at least part of your room decor is to acquire something living other than plants. Gerbils are well-known classroom standbys, snakes and ant farms less common. You will have to be sure, of course, that there will be no difficulties in caring for the creatures. During the wintertime, a classroom inhabitant can get very cold at night in northern climes.

Another theme that may serve your classroom is that of a particular country and its culture. You may want to remember this when you are on vacation. This is even more effective when you can have a film or outside speaker to tie in with your decorating efforts.

Whatever you choose to do to make your classroom more interesting and more enhancing to your subject area will be appreciated by your students and yourself. Remember, though, that you will want to redo your room in some way throughout the year. The same thing can get boring after a sufficient length of time. And eventually the students simply stop seeing what is around them.

EXERCISE

Check the calendar on pages 128–131 and choose at least 3 times in the year when you might want to redecorate your room. List what materials you would use.

AUDIO-VISUAL EQUIPMENT IN THE CLASSROOM

The classroom environment is part of an audio-visual approach to teaching. The more customary view of A-V, though, is to think in terms of equipment. You should find out early in the school year what audio-visual machines are available to you, and the wheres and hows of borrowing the equipment. Plan for using A-V machines. Depending on your subject area and grade level, they can be utilized in a number of different ways.

Tape recorders and tape players

Foreign language and language arts teachers have long been aware of the advantages to a class in playing or recording tapes. They can also be utilized in other subject areas. Tape players can help individualize learning or even testing. Listening centers can be plugged into tape recorders to serve one child or a small group wearing earphones. Think of these possibilities for tape recorder/players: short extra-credit quizzes, lectures that may have been missed by absentees, practice in listening skills such as following oral directions, student recording of stories/dramas. In addition, tape recorders may be used in conjunction with filmstrips or slide projectors.

Filmstrips and slide projectors

In your school you will probably find a number of filmstrips. They are available on practically every subject under the sun. Some filmstrips have a printed narrative. Others are accompanied by a taped narration. This taped narration, by the way, may have a small "ting" at intervals. Its purpose is to indicate to you that the matching filmstrip should be advanced to the next frame. Some filmstrip projectors have a player built into the machine. In this case you may find that the tape will automatically trigger an advancing of the film.

Slide projectors are not quite as versatile as filmstrips, although some teachers prefer them. With slides the teacher controls the rate of advance and the narration. In addition, teachers can easily develop their own slide collections and presentations.

All-in-one filmstrip/tape player machines

A comparative newcomer to this area is the filmstrip/tape machine that does not require a screen. It looks much like a television set and projects the picture on its own screen. This type of machine is an asset to a "learning corner" or in a lab situation. The screen is not big enough to be effective in large-class use ordinarily.

Television and radio sets

Time was when the corridors of education echoed with enthusiastic cheers for classroom media use. Listening to a radio or watching television can be of value, but this is rarely done now on a regular basis. Sometimes reception in a school building can be poor. Sometimes educators (and parents, too) feel that students should be participants rather than spectators of learning. And often there are simply not enough good programs available.

You may feel differently about this, particularly if you know of something worthwhile broadcast during the day which your class might ordinarily miss. Be cautious about radio use, though. Most youngsters have been too accustomed to television viewing to be able to concentrate their attention on a nonvisual program. You may have to preteach this listening skill.

Movie projectors

It is the rare school that does not have at least one movie projector. As to what you can show with it, try your local library. It may have not only its own collection of films but access to a lending film library. Local colleges, governmental offices and large companies are also likely sources of free films. Be sure to preview any unknown material, of course. Besides being deadly dull, it may be inappropriate for your grade level.

Overhead projectors

Overhead projectors may be ugly and ungainly looking, but some teachers count them as important as chalk and eraser. An overhead projector immediately solves the teacher's back-to-the-class problem. With an overhead you can face your group, write and look for reactions at the same time. Overhead projectors use commercially printed transparencies which you can mark up with grease pencils or waterbased ink pens. In addition you can use blank transparencies, or create your own with a Thermofax machine. You can use a transparency with blanks on it, then overlay it with a transparency that fills the blanks. If a Thermofax machine is available to you, you can use one piece of paper to create a transparency and a duplicating master. Overhead projectors, while versatile, are simple to work, with few moving parts.

Screens and substitutes

Projectors require something on which to project. The usual device is a screen made of relatively fragile material. Some teachers are lucky enough to have a screen above the black-board on a windowshade sort of arrangement. Others must depend on a collapsible tripod-based affair that sometimes has a diabolical mind of its own. If you are having difficulty acquiring or using a regular screen, think about alternatives. You can use the white back of a large wall map or bring an old sheet or white tablecloth or bedspread from home.

Musical instruments

The primary grade teacher is ordinarily familiar with the use of musical instruments in the room. Most of us can remember taking our turns in the rhythm band or the musical chairs of kindergarten. But there is no restriction on the use of musical instruments at any grade level, particularly in language learning. Performing musical interludes for a student play and teaching pronunciation through songs are just two of a range of activities in which you might use your talent. If you do play an instrument, such as a guitar, explore in your own mind its possibilities in your classroom.

Using, storing, and servicing
A-V equipment

Before you use any A-V equipment in front of a class, try it out in private. The bulb that needs replacing, the unfamiliar controls that need practicing with, or the height adjustment with which you must fiddle are all possible pitfalls. Material to be shown or heard should also be checked out carefully. Film gets scratched, sprockets get broken, and even almost foolproof tape cassettes can suddenly spew forth.

When you must store equipment in your room, be sure it is carefully put away. Even if a student knocks something down and breaks it, yours is the ultimate responsibility. Don't place temptation in the way of others, either. Store your equipment in a cupboard that locks.

Schools which use A-V equipment ordinarily have someone in charge of it. That person should be told when a machine does not work properly. If it cannot be easily fixed, the school probably has some sort of service contract for its repair.

SUMMARY

1. Audio-visual environment includes the classroom itself.
2. Plan your classroom decor carefully and use whatever low-cost materials are available.
3. Be familiar with the scope of A-V machines and use them.

HOMEWORK

Below you will find drawings of the four walls of a typical classroom. Choose a central theme related to a familiar subject and grade level. Furnish the room with specific materials. If you have difficulty finding a theme, check the Room Calendar on pages 128–131.

ROOM CALENDAR

SEPTEMBER
Monthlong—Fall, American Heritage, Back-to-School
3 Henry Hudson discovered the Hudson River
6 Jane Addams was born
10 Elias Howe patented the first sewing machine
11 O. Henry (William Sydney Porter) was born
16 The Mayflower sailed from Plymouth, England
18 George Washington laid cornerstone of the Capitol
23 Zodiac sign of Libra begins
26 Daniel Boone died

OCTOBER
Monthlong—Harvest, Hallowe'en, Indian Summer
8 The Great Chicago Fire began
10 Helen Hayes was born
12 Columbus Day
17 Noah Webster was born
19 The National Anthem was sung for the first time (Baltimore)
22 The Metropolitan Opera opened
23 Zodiac sign of Scorpio begins
24 Anna Edson Taylor survived going over
        Niagara Falls in a barrel
27 Theodore Roosevelt was born
29 The start of the 1930s depression
31 Hallowe'en

NOVEMBER
Monthlong—Pilgrims, Thanksgiving
2 Daniel Boone was born
   Marie Antoinette was born
4 FDR became the first and only president
        elected to a third term
7 Marie Curie was born
   First Tuesday–Election Day
11 Veteran's Day (formerly Armistice Day)
14 Horse-drawn streetcars appeared in New York City
18 The U.S. adopted Standard time throughout

19 Gettysburg Address
22 Zodiac sign of Saggitarius begins
26 First official Thanksgiving Day celebration in U.S.
29 Louisa May Alcott was born
30 Mark Twain (Samuel Clemens) was born
   4th Thursday-Thanksgiving

DECEMBER
Monthlong—Winter, Channukah, Christmas
 2 The first savings bank opened in Philadelphia
 6 Death of St. Nicholas
 7 Delaware ratified the Constitution (first state to do so)
 8 AFL was founded
10 Emily Dickinson was born
14 George Washington died
16 Boston Tea Party
17 First successful flight at Kitty Hawk by Wright brothers
21 First day of winter
22 Zodiac sign of Capricorn begins
25 Christmas
28 W.F. Semple patented chewing gum

JANUARY
Monthlong—Winter, New Year
 6 Twelfth Night, Epiphany, or Three Kings Day
 7 First presidential election in the U.S.
11 Birth of Eugenio Maria de Hostos
12 Horatio Alger was born
15 Birth of Martin Luther King, Jr.
19 Robert E. Lee was born
20 Zodiac sign of Aquarius begins
22 Death of Queen Victoria after sixty-four years as monarch
24 James W. Marshall discovered gold in California
25 Nelly Bly circled the world in seventy-two days
26 *Hans Brinker* author, Mary Mapes Dodge, was born
26 Birth of Juan Pablo Duarte
28 Birth of José Marti
29 W.C. Fields was born
31 Betsy Ross died

FEBRUARY

Monthlong—Presidents, Valentine's Day, Leap Year
Variable: Beginning of Lent:
Mardi Gras or Shrove Tuesday

12 Lincoln's birthday
13 Oldest public school in America (Boston) opened
14 Valentine's Day
15 Susan B. Anthony was born
18 Discovery of Pluto, ninth planet, in 1930
19 Thomas A. Edison patented phonograph
   Zodiac sign of Pisces begins
20 John Glenn orbited world three times in 1962
22 Washington's birthday
23 Samuel Pepys was born
   John Keats died

MARCH

Monthlong—Spring, Flowers

2 Congress established the General Post Office
3 Alexander Graham Bell was born
7 Luther Burbank was born
9 Amerigo Vespucci was born
10 *Uncle Tom's Cabin* was published
11 Johnny Appleseed (John Chapman) died
12 Juliette Low founded Girl Scouts
14 Albert Einstein was born
17 St. Patrick's Day
19 Day swallows return to Capistrano
21 Zodiac sign of Aries begins
21 Birth of Benito Juárez
26 Jonas Salk announced his anti-polio vaccine
27 Ponce de Leon discovered Florida
28 Nathaniel Briggs patented a washing machine (1797)
30 Purchase of Alaska (1867)

APRIL

Monthlong—Spring, Flowers, Easter/Passover

1 April Fool's Day (kept alive largely by school children.
  N.B. teachers)

1 Beginning of National Laugh Week
3 First Pony Express
5 Pocahontas married John Rolfe
9 Robert E. Lee surrendered
12 Clara Barton died
13 Thomas Jefferson was born
15 Abraham Lincoln was assassinated
17 Benjamin Franklin died
18 Paul Revere's ride
20 Zodiac sign of Taurus begins
30 George Washington inaugurated

MAY
Monthlong—Gardens, Mothers
Movable—Mother's Day, second Sunday
6 Sigmund Freud was born
15 Nylon stockings were sold for the first time (1940)
16 First Oscars awarded
19 Birth of Malcolm X
21 Charles Lindbergh flew solo transatlantic to Paris
23 Kit Carson died
24 Brooklyn Bridge opened (1883)
27 Amelia Bloomer was born
30 Memorial Day
31 Johnstown Flood (1889)

JUNE
Monthlong—Summer, Vacation, Fathers
Movable—Father's Day, second Sunday
3 Jefferson Davis was born
5 Franklin flew his kite, precursor of lightning rod
14 Flag Day
19 Statue of Liberty arrived in the U.S. from France
25 Custer's last stand
26 Opening of Atlantic City boardwalk
27 Helen Keller was born
28 Molly Pitcher fought in Battle of Monmouth
29 First airplane flight between California and Hawaii
30 Congress passed Pure Food and Drug Act

Open Bookcase

Bulletin Board

Closed Bookcase

Closed Bookcases

EAST WALL

Bulletin Boards over Clothes Closets

SOUTH WALL

			Bulletin Board						Bulletin Board
Windows				W i n d o w s					

Windowsills - 6 inches wide

Radiators

NORTH WALL

Frieze - 12 inches wide

Blackboard

Plain Paneling

WEST WALL

PART THREE
DEALING WITH OTHERS AND YOURSELF

CHAPTER TEN

SUPERVISORS AND OTHER SCHOOL PERSONNEL

KEEPING YOUR PRINCIPALS IN MIND

AIMS

1. To understand what supervisors expect and why.
2. To consider the role of out-of-class school personnel.
3. To develop a basis for your attitude toward other teachers.

MOTIVATION

Today is Ms. P's first observation. Her supervisor, Mr. X, enters the classroom and seats himself in the back. For about ten minutes he makes quiet notes, then as quietly, gets up and leaves. Ms. P feels awkward and resentful. Her lesson was building to a climax, and now Mr. X won't be there to see.

YOU AND THE SUPERVISOR

To most teachers a supervisor seems a natural enemy. The usual attitude is that a supervisor combines the most disliked elements of a boss and a parent. Many teachers feel that schools would be better places with fewer supervisors.

There are obvious reasons for this stance. Teachers are, in a sense, graded by supervisors. Supervisors are the ones who request, suggest, order, and cajole. On the other hand, part of the teachers' traditional attitude probably arises from the fact that the supervisor is regarded as an "outsider" in the classroom, an intruder on a situation which the teacher is accustomed to dominating.

It may help you generally if you remember that the student, not the teacher, is the center of the classroom. When you truly believe this, you will discover that with this view you and the supervisor are allies rather than adversaries, a far easier position from which to deal with your relationships.

The job of supervisor is to help you be a more effective teacher. There are various aspects to this job, but the most obvious one is to observe you in the classroom and discuss that observation with you. Indeed, some teachers feel that this is the main occupation of the supervisor. Yet supervisors in general maintain that they are not free to do this activity enough. Wherever the truth lies, it is inevitable that you will be observed once or many times during the year.

OBSERVATIONS

The classic observation technique includes a pre-conference between teacher and supervisor. At this conference are discussed the upcoming lesson, the lesson plan, and even specifics of what the supervisor may be seeking. This pre-observation conference is honored more in the breach than in the reality, but if it does occur in your case, there are at least two things to remember. The first is that you have every right to ask the supervisor to observe a particular lesson or class as long as your request is reasonable, for example, that you are teaching something with which you have difficulty, or conversely, with which you have had success. An unreasonable request is that since the students in a particular class are difficult to discipline, you would rather not be observed in that situation.

A second thing to remember is that you can take advantage of an observation to find out not only about your teaching but about your students. Whether your supervisor appears sympathetic or not, he or she is a trained observer. Now is the time to see what someone else makes of Nelly's lack of attention or Evita's hyperactivity. It is very difficult to teach a group of students and concentrate closely on one member of the group. You are entitled to ask your supervisor's help in this.

Whether you have a preobservation conference or not, you will certainly be required to discuss your lesson plan with your supervisor. This is not an exquisite form of torture. It is a sound basis for the supervisor's understanding of what you are trying to do. Some supervisors ask to see the lesson plan after an observation, others require it ahead of time. Here your legibility and organization will definitely count.

Sometimes supervisors prefer to announce that they will be visiting you. Other times you will look up from the attendance list and find that there is an extra body in your classroom. Be very careful of your initial reaction—not for your supervisor's sake but for that of the students. While you may want to welcome the supervisor, keep it low key and continue your usual activities. The students will know someone else is in the room anyhow, so why dwell on it?

A word to the wise about your students when you are being observed: You will be astonished to find that they immediately align themselves with you. Hands that are never raised an inch above desktop are suddenly waving in the air. Even someone who has not responded before will come to life. Your students will probably do everything in their power to make you look good, wise and interesting.

One technique that some teachers enjoy is that of involving the supervisor in the lesson itself. You may not want to abdicate the entire class period, but you can sometimes turn the visit into a broadened experience for the students when you hand over your chalk for a few minutes. There are supervisors who refuse to be drawn into the lesson. They feel that their role must be neutral, and this is probably true. But there is no harm in referring a student question, with a smile, to your visitor.

Supervisors in observing you will be looking for certain things, obvious ones when you consider them. First, they will be checking the thrust of your lesson. Are its aims possible with this group? Did the motivation interest the students? Did your plan carry through for the entire class period? They will also be seeking to find how you handle students. Whom did you call on, and how often? Did anyone appear to be lagging behind or dominating? If so, what did you do about it? Finally the supervisor will probably look at students' written work—the notebook or section of the notebook kept on classwork, the homework, the boardwork—and how you correct it or have students correct it. Some supervisors will also be checking the physical environment of your room, although the day is long past when an important observation criterion was the even level of all window shades.

Whether you were involved in a preobservation discussion or not, there will be a conference and/or letter after the event. With most supervisors there will be a recap of what you planned to do, an in-depth coverage of what happened in the lesson itself, then some suggestions on what can be done to improve or expand what you are doing. During this conference, you may be defensive or just plain nervous, but try to control this tendency. If teaching students is what you are paid to do, then helping you teach better is the motive for your supervisor's salary. Open your mind as well as your ears, and you may learn something to your teaching advantage. On the other hand, if you feel that the suggestions for improvement are inappropriate, try them once and then discard them if they are not helpful. What may work for someone else may not do so for you. Supervisors understand that also.

OTHER CONTACTS

Supervisors do more than observe teachers. You may be required by your supervisor to prepare reports, hand in lesson plans, have material to be duplicated be preapproved, and even do some research perhaps. Some of this will seem suspiciously like busywork, but that may not be your supervisor's fault. Some of the work, such as handing in a sample batch of graded tests, may be designed to keep the supervisor regularly in touch with what you are doing. Other work may be something the system itself requires.

You will also be receiving letters and memos from supervisors. It might be well to set up some sort of system for yourself on memos that deal with due dates for such things as book receipts or grades. It could be as simple as a file folder or as elegant as a commercially made file book with sections for each day. Some of the material may not be worth keeping once you have read it. If you dispose of it in the wastebasket file, it is more politic to do so when your supervisor is not around. Some letters may have to be answered, particularly ones that are placed in your permanent file. Even if you are not asked for an answer, you may want to reply, and that is ordinarily your right. Do, though, write something other than a hasty scrawl on scrap paper.

Supervisors have meetings that you will be expected to attend. Some are more interesting than others. Even in the dullest conference, you can still gain teaching skill. There you will learn why children squirm in class and whisper to one another while you are teaching. In short, while many meetings seem tediously long, you can exercise your good manners and understanding.

Just as there is no law that says you must like every single one of your students, there is none mandating that you and your supervisor must be kindred souls. Since we are all people with a varying mix of qualities, we respond to others according to our own views. You may have a supervisor who is, in your opinion, too old-fashioned, or conversely, too "progressive." That supervisor may ask you to do some things in the classroom with which you do not agree. According to your school or system, you may not be able to refuse. If that is the case, then do what you have been asked with as much grace as possible. If you feel the material or technique is not succeeding, go back to your supervisor and discuss what you think will work. It is probable that you will be given a chance to try out your ideas. Whatever the tension between you, though, remember that you and your supervisor are in agreement on one issue: Students should learn.

EXERCISE

Mr. M is a fifth grade teacher whose supervisor, Ms. A, believes that reading, 'riting and 'rithmetic should be emphasized above all else. Ms. A has told Mr. M that he must concentrate on these basic skills even at the cost of losing time from such areas as art and music. Mr. M feels that children need creative outlets. Are there any ways he can accommodate Ms. A and still hold true to his ideals?

OTHER SCHOOL PERSONNEL

The general public thinks of a school as a place for students, teachers, and supervisors. You, as an insider, will soon find that other school personnel can have a deep effect on your life as a teacher. While the particular personnel employed in every school system may vary, you will generally have contact with such people as: secretaries, school nurses, guidance counselors, librarians, cafeteria workers, custodians, and aides outside the classroom.

School secretaries are influential people. Depending on local procedures, your school's secretary may keep track of personnel data (absence, lateness, time-in and time-out, credentials); student body data (registration, attendance statistics, transfers, withdrawals, permanent records; finances (typing orders for books and materials, managing bank accounts, and maintaining petty cash); clerical work (receiving dictation and typing memos, letters, forms, reports, observations, logs); and reception duties (visitors, phone calls, deliveries). The position of school secretary can be a highly skilled one. Some systems require college credits or a degree for the post. Almost invariably, though, schools pay their secretaries less than those in private industry. You may have excellent relations with the secretarial personnel in your school. If you don't, you might remember that the job is a demanding one and usually underpaid.

School nurses in many states never have a chance to nurse. Some states have clear regulations forbidding nurses to dispense any medication—even aspirin. Anything more complicated than a cold compress must be referred off school grounds. Nurses must, though, keep detailed records. Most of the time they rely on you, as teacher, to supply them with the needed material. Inoculations take place over a period of years, and it is quite likely that a child will suddenly hand you a slip from the doctor. If your mind is on the mass of other responsibilities you have, you may put the slip away and tend to forget it. Don't do so. You are making someone else's job harder.

Guidance counselors are another group of out-of-classroom personnel whose work is intertwined with yours. Many are former teachers and so have an understanding of your situation. All will be in need of information from you at one time or another. Make sure that information is complete and factual rather than spotty and subjective because counselors must work with various agencies who require reports that may run to several pages. Counselors usually have something to do with articulation—the movement of students from one school to a higher level. Some function as career counselors. Some do informal counseling. It is a potpourri sort of job which may or may not include relieving you of classroom miscreants. Early in your experience in any school, it is important for you to acquaint yourself with guidance personnel and their specific duties.

School librarians should be teachers. They should, at the very least, work with teachers to provide children not only with books but with experience in using a library. Unfortunately, this is one area in which school boards find it easy to cut back. Some schools have libraries but no specialized personnel. Others don't even have libraries but rely on local out-of-school facilities. If you are in a school with both a full-fledged library and librarian, cherish them both. You will find them an invaluable resource for yourself (ask for the professional journals) and for your class. Some librarians whose classroom experience has been limited are nervous about hordes descending upon them. Make sure when you take your students into the library that they have been told what type of behavior is expected of them. Even in the library you are their teacher and responsible for them.

Facilities for student eating in a school range from a specialized lunchroom to a large area that changes roles according to the time of day; however, most schools serve the food cafeteria-style. Cafeteria personnel may not be in your classroom, but they do have direct contact with your students. It is possible that you will have direct contact with them also in this nonclassroom setting if you have cafeteria duty. Cafeteria personnel from dietician to soup-server do not have easy lives. You will observe this if you have noontime duty. If there is a seamier side of education, this has to be it. The child who is demurely subservient in your room turns into a tiger when confronted with tapioca pudding. Treble voices loudly reject perfectly acceptable if rather mundane food. Hideous fates await cooked prunes. Somehow though, even with all these negative forces, some cafeteria personnel remain calm and friendly. If they don't, remember that their lot is usually not a happy one.

If you care for mottos, you might memorize: Cooperate with custodians, and they will cooperate with you. Custodial personnel have a subtle but pervasive effect on your classroom life. If there is a broken window, lost key, burnt-out lightbulb or souvenir of a stomach virus, you will quickly learn that it is important to have good personal relations with the custodian. You can do so by keeping your classroom easy to clean, chairs on tables at day's end for example. You can also do so simply by being friendly. People are more inclined to be helpful toward those whom they like.

Some systems employ school aides who do not work in the classroom. They may be office helpers, security guards, attendance workers, mimeograph room personnel. Here again you will do well to be friendly. A school is not just a physical entity. It is an interplay of personalities. The better relationships that exist among all school personnel, the better the atmosphere will be for everyone.

EXERCISE

Think of a job you have held either in a large organization or in a large building. List the people whose work was peripheral to yours. How many names did you know? What difference could it have meant to you in your position?

OTHER TEACHERS

Besides supervisors and out-of-classroom school personnel, there is a whole group of people whose attitude toward you as a teacher and yours toward them can be influential. These are the other teachers in your school. Whether your school is small or large, other teachers can have an effect on your feelings toward yourself, your students and the organization itself.

In your teaching career you will encounter good, bad and, indifferent teachers. It might be well to prepare yourself for those encounters. You should be ready to learn from all experiences, and you will learn from others who are involved in the same situation as you are. Most teachers are helpful to one another. Sometimes, though, you will run across certain types who will not be helpful.

Most schools have one or more "old" teachers. By this is meant not the chronologically old, but the old in experience. Usually an experienced teacher is delighted to lend at least a shoulder to cry on to the newest pedagogues. Every now and then, however, you will find an experienced teacher who is unfriendly to you and to your ideas. When you think about it, the reasons may become clear. You could appear to the experienced teacher as a challenge to security. Perhaps the teacher went through a great deal of trial and error in the beginning and feels it is only just that you do so, too. The experienced teacher may seem cool to you because there are pressures and problems outside the school of which you may not be aware. Or the teacher in question may be a person who is generally reserved with everyone. You may react to an unfriendly person by being pretty unfriendly yourself. That is your privilege. On the other hand, you gain nothing by either feeling guilty ("It must have been something I did") or becoming aggressive ("By heaven, I'll make that teacher pay attention to me").

Closely allied with and sometimes overlapping the experienced teacher is another type, the jealous one. The jealous teacher is often hard to spot because the jealousy may be covered up with flattering compliments. Jealousy rises from a feeling of inadequacy, and there is not much you can do to predict why you should make another teacher feel inadequate. Reasons can run the spectrum from physical attractiveness to popularity with students. When you have a co-worker who is fulsome about your talents, remember that flattery always contains an element of surprise. And if you do determine that someone is jealous of you, remember that in itself is a sort of compliment.

The gossiping teacher is another person to be aware of. Schools, like other organizations where people work closely together, are sometimes hotbeds of rumor. While it is pleasant to think yourself in the know, it is also a possible source of embarrassment. If you don't care for gossip, avoid the teachers who do so like the plague. And remember, for every time they talk to you about someone else, there is probably an instance when they tell someone else about you.

A final type of teacher whom you may meet somewhere during schooltime is the overprotective one. This teacher is not overprotective of you but of your students. This is the teacher who does not tell you about misbehavior among your pupils, not because of the fear that you will punish them, but because the teacher wants to be "friends" with the students. This is a dangerous and unhealthy attitude. If you observe it in another, you should see that someone in authority is aware of it. If you observe it in yourself, start thinking about your relationships with students. Overprotectiveness never taught the fledgling to fly. At an advanced age we would still be sitting waiting for someone to feed us if someone else didn't force us to try our wings. Your students will never be helped by an overprotective teacher, whether it is you or another.

The previous catalog of fellow teacher types is, unfortunately, all negative. It is impossible to list the many positive types of relationships you will have. Yet they will be the majority of your experiences with co-workers. You will find professional guidance, personal friendship, and a desire to help you in most of the teachers of every school. The quick word in the corridor, the smile across the auditorium, the hastily-shared sandwich, the chat after 3 p.m. will mean more to you as a teacher and person than any of the bad encounters. Teaching, as parenting, can bring out the best as well as the worse in us.

SUMMARY

I. Supervisors must supervise. Expect a relationship that includes

  A. Observations—preparation, lesson and discussion afterwards
  B. Assigning work, writing letters, memos and conducting meetings
  C. Day-to-day contact and instructions

II. You should be aware of and know the value of other school personnel such as secretaries, nurses, guidance counselors, librarians, cafeteria workers, custodial help and school aides.

III. Other teachers can be helpful or not. Some negative types are
A. The "old" teacher
B. The jealous teacher
C. The gossip
D. The overprotective teacher

HOMEWORK

Below is the organization of a typical middle-sized school. Choose four people and write a paragraph about each. Describe them briefly and tell what you think their attitude would be toward you and yours toward them. Draw on your own experience in schools and elsewhere.

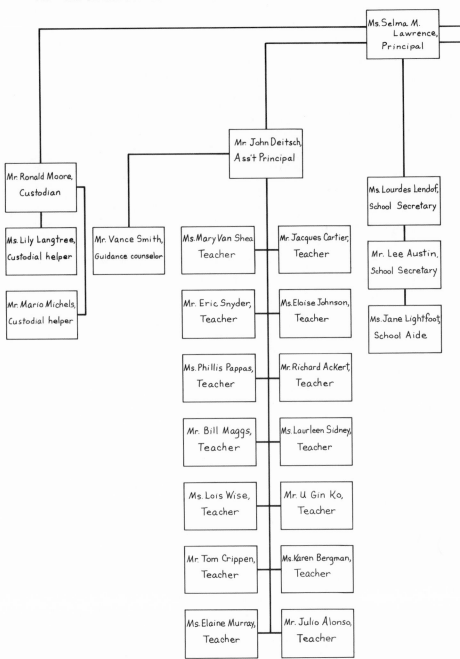

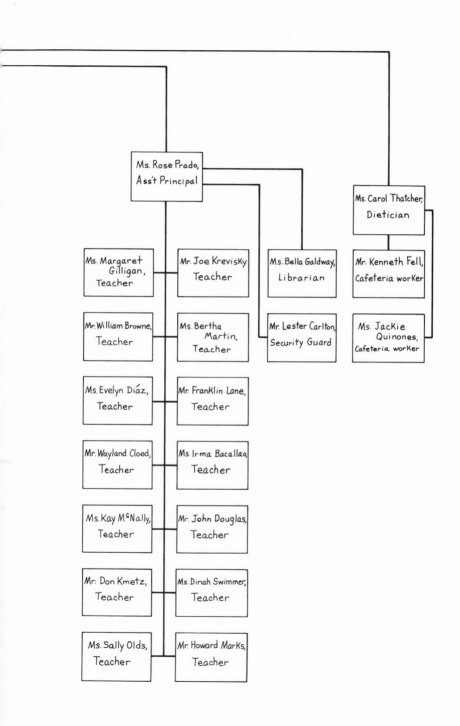

CHAPTER ELEVEN

PARENTS AND COMMUNITY

SHE'S SUCH
AN UNUSUAL CHILD

AIMS

1. To consider why and how a parent's viewpoint differs from the teacher's.
2. To understand how to effectively communicate with parents.
3. To develop a professional attitude toward all community relationships.

DO NOW

List the varying segments of the community which are in contact with the school or influence it. You should be able to think of at least four.

MOTIVATION

Ms. Webster has come to school in answer to a letter from the teacher of her daughter Sara. The teacher is busy at her desk writing. After a minute or so Ms. Webster clears her throat. The teacher looks up inquiringly, and Ms. Webster says, "I'm Sara's mother." "Sara?" says the teacher blankly. Ms. Webster thinks resentfully, at least she could know my daughter's name.

TEACHERS AND PARENTS ARE DIFFERENT

A teacher can be a parent, but a parent is not a teacher. A parent's role is very different from that of a teacher. Usually a parent's concept of a child is very different, also. This is only logical. You as teacher see the child as a student, one of an entire class. Children in a group do not behave as they would by themselves ordinarily. The leader, the follower, the bully, the loudmouth, and the meek are all playing parts that relate to their peers. At home the child is one of a much smaller group, some of whom are not peers but of an older generation. This fact underlies much misunderstanding between parents and teachers. A mother who sees her son on a one-to-one basis may have difficulty understanding what he is like as a student in a class. A father who finds his daughter lively and talkative may be stunned if you tell him that she is withdrawn from others in school.

It is also important to realize that aside from the different behavior a child may display in school than at home, you must allow for gaps between your ability to control behavior in the classroom and the parent's ability to do so. This knife cuts two ways. You may find a child among other children easier to deal with than the parent. Or sometimes, because of a different standard, the parent may have less difficulty than you.

Finally, there is a wide gap between you and the parent in the emotional relationship with the child. For various reasons parents are generally very fond of their offspring. Some of these reasons arise from the parent's concept of self which identifies with children's achievements or failures. You as a teacher may be fond of a student and take great pleasure and credit in that student's achievement, but you know that your own success or failure does not depend on one child alone. The parent simply cannot be as objective as you are.

In order to communicate effectively with parents, you must first accept that your viewpoints of children are divergent. With this in mind, you must also consider that your experiences are divergent. In many families both parents work, but that work is generally not school-connected. The idiom that you speak with others in education is a foreign language to most parents. Schools run on a different timetable and yearly schedule than most businesses. Knowledge of child growth and learning processes that you may take for granted could be more specialized than you realize.

Much confusion between parents and teachers could be

avoided by the teacher's understanding and allowing for their naturally differing points of view. Take a common teacher-parent contact, the telephone call. The circumstances under which the parent receives that call can make it effective or an exercise in futility. If you make the call during school hours you may reach a parent at home for various reasons—no occupation outside the house, illness, nighttime job hours. If you need to call at night, you may be interrupting a meal, a family argument, entertainment, or even an early bedtime. At any time your call may be an intrusion. If it is your job to contact the home, of course you must do so, but future conversation can be smoothed by a quick identification of yourself and the question, "Is it convenient to talk now or would you prefer me to call back later?"

Your time is valuable and so is the parent's. Before you telephone the family, make sure you know the exact points you want to cover. Some parents may want to discuss something other than what you had in mind. It is easy to go off on a tangent and never return to the one area you wanted to bring up. Some parents may want to talk longer than you feel necessary. In that case, you might suggest that you must call others and will be glad to have a personal conference in school at a specific time to go more thoroughly into the parent's concerns.

A teacher-parent letter is another manifestation of the differences between roles. You as teacher may write to the parent to inform, to question, or to ask for help. Whatever your purpose, the letter will have the stamp of officialdom simply because it comes from the student's school. If you mail the letter, it can arrive with a stack of bills as more bad news. Some people react to bad news by postponement. Your letter may not be answered right away. In some households a letter from school may be considered automatic disgrace. No matter what your purpose for writing, the student will be punished. If a letter is sent home with a student or even mailed to an address where a child has access to the mailbox, the parent may not receive your missive. Many teachers have felt a parent uncooperative and unresponsive when the parent was not even aware that a letter had been sent.

Parent-teacher conferences in school are also events with

changeable meanings according to each participant. The teacher is usually concerned about making certain points within a limited time. The parent, on the other hand, wants to feel that sufficient attention and concern is being given to the student's situation. You will want to prepare for a parent-teacher conference not only by noting matters to be discussed, but also by arranging a quiet place where you can talk as long as possible with the parent. If a parent comes to school unannounced to talk with you and you are busy, arrange a convenient date for later, but be sure that the parents know why you cannot confer right then and there. And if help is available to take over your class, it may be well worth your while to drop what you are doing and sit down with the parent privately. Some unplanned conferences are extremely important because you will learn of emergency conditions or deep-seated concerns that might not appear in an orchestrated meeting.

TALKING TO PARENTS

While the difference in viewpoint is important to you in arranging conferences, making phone calls, or sending letters, it is perhaps most vital in considering how you talk and what you say in those letters, conferences, and calls. Aside from the usual desire of human beings to be liked, more can be accomplished when the parents think of you in a positive rather than negative way.

To parents their children are unique. Remember that when you are talking or writing to them. To you a child may be seen in comparison and contrast to others. This may lead you to say, "Fulano is one of those children who . . ." and feel that this demonstrates your professional experience. To the parent it shows that you are grouping Fulano with students whose behavior, academic or otherwise, is none of the parent's concern.

When you talk to parents, say things that they will accept on an emotional level, yet understand on a nonemotional one. Parents understand that a student is in school to learn. They may or may not understand that a student cannot learn well when she or he is ill, tired, distracted, or discouraged, but if they do not know, you can tell them this and they will generally listen.

Parents can understand that homework is important to a child's learning, and, if you explain it, they are ready to learn that there are different kinds of homework. Parents understand that students who are better educated are better prepared for life. Unless you tell them, they may not realize that encouraging responsibility, effort and other sterling character qualities also prepares students for the workaday world. All of these areas are pertinent and nonemotional enough to serve as bases for discussion between you and parents.

That discussion should be in plain, ordinary language, whether English or not. (When you have a parent who does not speak your language, be sure the translation is done by someone sensitive to nuances, hopefully not a child. There can be real damage in the choice of one word over another.) There have been schools and systems which circulate lists of "acceptable" phrases to use in parent-teacher conferences. Most lists bristle with the circumlocution of educationese, i.e., "inappropriate," "nonachievement," "living skills." The purpose of most of these lists is not to make the situation clearer to the parent but to protect the teacher from "inappropriate" language. Most teachers already know that there is no positive value in telling a parent that a child is bad, stupid, lazy, or obnoxious. There are other ways of expressing the truth without resorting to obfuscation. You can say, "Emil does not behave as he should. He talks when he shouldn't. He teases other children sometimes. He needs to know that you as a parent do not approve of this kind of behavior." Even the most protective parent will be able to see what the problem is, which is the first step in solving it.

Do think about what you will say to a particular parent before you say it. Especially in a letter, you will want to appear professional (no misspellings), unprejudiced (no words with emotional connotations) and open to suggestion (not "I think" but "Do you think"). In talking with a parent, *never* compare or contrast a child unfavorably with others in the class, disclose your familiarity with intimate family matters, attempt to place blame on the family, or depart from facts into speculation.

Add your own words to describe student behavior to the list below. Review the list and find substitutes for any words that may have a negative effect on a parent.

Some Frank but Polite Language to Use with Parents

Don't Say	*Do Say:*
"He or she behaves badly"	"He or she talks" . . . throws spitballs" . . . doesn't obey"
"He or she is a bully"	"He or she pulls other children's hair" . . . frightens other children" . . . takes money from other children"
"He or she steals or robs"	"He or she took_____without asking"
"He or she is lazy"	"He or she must work harder" . . . must do work on time" . . . correctly" . . . neatly"
"He or she is rude or defiant"	"He or she said, '_____' when I asked him or her to_____"
"He or she is not intelligent"	"He or she has trouble with academic work" . . . does not under- stand easily" . . . needs extra help at home and school"
"He or she is spoiled"	"He or she expects special attention" . . . should behave more maturely" . . . must learn to get along as one of a group"

OTHER COMMUNITY PEOPLE

Parents of children in your classroom are not the only members of the community who may have some involvement with education, your school, and you. At one time or another, you will probably be in contact with school volunteers, members of the parents' association, and with the school board.

Usually your contact with school volunteers is closest when there are parent volunteers in your classroom. Remember that while you are at home in your room, volunteers are not. It is part of your job to welcome them, provide space for their work, and, if necessary, give direction. Some schools have parent volunteers at a desk at the entrance. Neither they nor the volunteers in your classroom are menials and should not be asked to do something for which they have not volunteered. In addition, most volunteers are parents who are not professional educators and may not be able to deal with a particular situation in the way that you would. It is not their fault but yours if you expect them to teach or behave like you do. Once you accept these limitations, you will find much to commend in the help that volunteers can give you.

Some parents' associations are more active than others. This may be due to the school's administration, to the economic demands of a neighborhood or to a lack of confidence in the parents themselves. A more active parents' association will have at least a monthly meeting, and you may be asked to attend or even to speak. If this occurs, remember again that you are dealing with people who are usually not professional educators. If you are tapped to explain a particular program, do it in terms that parents can understand. Parents in general want to know what is happening in school and how they can help children at home. They are probably not interested in the theories and research of your field unless directly related to the reality of their children here and now.

Aside from attending meetings, you may find the parents' association of your school involved in organizing faculty-parent committees, encouraging academic achievement through awards or scholarships, and providing extra money or helping hands for special projects and programs. If you have the child of a parents' association officer in your class, you may even tend to see the group from an uneasily personal point of view. All or none of this can happen depending on your school and system, but be aware of the possibilities.

The same holds true for school boards. Some boards or board members are far more involved in the day-to-day activities of schools than others. You may find it necessary to attend an open board meeting, and perhaps even to speak. Remember that your audience, though more likely to include professional educators, will come primarily from fields outside of yours. Some members of school boards think of education in basically dollars-and-cents terms. After all, that may be the reason they were elected or appointed. Some board members may be in that position through a desire for power. Others may feel that the position entitles them to an automatic superiority of knowledge over yours. These are political facts of life. Your position as a teacher vis-à-vis the school board may have much to do with events of which you are not aware. It is probably best in planning any personal contact with the board to discuss the ramifications with those more familiar with the situation, a supervisor, or other teachers.

In your life as a teacher you may well have minimal contacts with volunteers, parents' associations, or school boards. But they exist, and they can have an influence over where, what, and how you teach. Do not ignore them. They are as much a part of the educational community as you are.

SUMMARY

1. Understand that a parent's viewpoint is different from yours and consider this in calling the home, writing letters, and holding conferences.

2. Since parents are different, be sure you are communicating clearly and factually. Plan beforehand what you will say and how to say it.

3. Be aware of other community contacts with the school: volunteers, parents' associations, and the school board.

HOMEWORK

Read the following and decide where you would have acted differently or not and how:

It is the middle of October, and already Ms. Lane knows that Elizabeth T. is this year's thorn in her side. Elizabeth is the youngest, largest and possibly brightest child in Ms. Lane's fourth grade class. She is also lazy, noisy, and sulky when reproofed. Ms. Lane has already written two letters home, and there has been no reply. Ms. Lane has called both at night and during the school day and no one has answered. Today during her prep period, Ms. Lane has been summoned to the office. There an imposing older woman introduces herself as Ms. T and says that she would like to talk about Elizabeth.

MS. LANE: I'm delighted to see you. I've been trying to get in touch with you for weeks about Elizabeth.

MS. T: Oh, really? I didn't get any letters.

MS. LANE: Maybe Elizabeth didn't show them to you, but I did send two.

MS. T: Elizabeth tells me everything. She wouldn't lie about something like that.

MS. LANE: I tried to call you, too, and there was never anyone home.

MS. T: My sister's been ill, and we've been living over there mostly, helping out. Listen. I wanted to talk to you because Elizabeth tells me you've been picking on her.

MS. LANE: Picking on her? Whatever gave her that idea?

MS. T: She told me you're after her constantly, and I don't like it. Elizabeth is a sweet little girl and that's not fair. Besides, I want you to know that we live next door to Mr. L who's on the school board, and I just might discuss this with him.

MS. T: Well, I wish you'd listen to my side of the story. Let's talk about it.

MS. LANE: You treat Elizabeth right, and you'll be OK. I don't understand why you teachers can't take it a little easier on the kids. After all, you're only young once, I always say.

CHAPTER TWELVE

THE SCHOOL YEAR

THANK GOD IT'S
MEMORIAL DAY

AIMS

1. To understand that the time rhythms in the education world are different from those in the rest of the working world
2. To mentally prepare for the ups and downs of the school year
3. To consider the options for your vacations

MOTIVATION

For the ninth time, Caroline's friend Sonia is talking about how lucky Caroline is. "You have all that time at Christmas and around Easter," she complains, "and the whole summer off. It's just not fair. You even work a shorter day than I do. I think teachers have it too easy." Caroline remembers the innumerable pressures of her first teaching year and wisely bites her tongue.

9 MONTHS VERSUS 12

Most businesses operate on a year-round basis. And since most people work in businesses, they too think in terms of a twelve-month year. Schoolteaching is different. While children may learn (and unlearn) all year, their formal education is usually a nine-month one. Some systems have discussed changing this. Indeed some have converted to a "full" school year although in reality it is usually three months on and one month off. In general, though, this has not been successful. It is most probable that you will teach from September through June, more or less. This fact has a profound influence on your sense of time.

Whereas most of the adult world celebrates the new year on the first of January, your year really begins somewhere around Labor Day. And September is a beginning for you in all the traditional ways—the resolutions, the sense of renewal, the casting off of the old. On the other hand, June puts a period to "this year's" experiences although most people do their end-year summing-up after Christmas. In addition, you as a teacher have a far clearer beginning and end to your year because of the lapse of at least two months between them.

But a nine-month versus a twelve-month year does present some problems. While critics of education blithely talk about the years children spend in school, they fail to point out that those years are shorter than calendar ones. The children in your class have only nine months in which to learn from you, a fact that puts you under special time pressures. For those secondary school teachers who have semester rather than full-year courses, the pressure is even greater.

Another negative aspect of a nine-month year is that holidays are usually pretty well spaced throughout that time with the exception of the weeks after Easter. And any teacher knows that the days immediately before and after holidays are almost always less productive than others. Sometimes there are special assemblies or parties, but even without them, children are restless beforehand and sluggish afterwards.

Finally, another disadvantage of the school year is the resentment it engenders in the bosoms of others. Caroline's friend Sonia is expressing something that you will hear or read again and again. The general public, most of whom have never faced a classroom full of students, feel that teachers have it "too good." The fact that teaching is qualitative rather than quantitative is rarely publicized. Teaching is intense, emotionally and physically exhausting work, but unfortunately only teachers know this. And they are usually much too busy to talk about it.

YEARLY PATTERNS

After the experience of teaching for some time, most people notice that there are patterns within the school year that define limits and sometimes make teaching easier or more difficult. One such pattern is the Report Card period. While a few places still issue grades at the end of each month, most systems now use a quarterly division for reporting. This means that grades are given in the beginning of November, at the end of January, in the middle of April, and at the end of the school year in June. Where semesters divide the year, the midway point is usually the beginning of February. Because it takes time for all the paraphernalia of report cards to be completed, you will be given a closing date for marks a few days or a week in advance. It is important to know what the report card periods are in your school because your planning must include the testing necessary to have a basis for student marks when they are expected.

A second pattern within the school year is less discernible but just as real. It is based on the fact that some parts of the school year can be more productive than others. You will, to a certain extent, set your own pattern, but most people find that it is about the same. In September, October, and November, you will see your students working hard. After Thanksgiving there will be a sudden slackening of effort. In January you can plunge in again, and if there is an intersession break in February, you will have the same experience. Somewhere in March or April everything sags. There is a slight improvement in May, but from the end of May until school closes, the same students who were models in the fall will be daydreaming. Some teachers new to the profession are unaware of these highs and lows in the school year and feel that they must be doing something wrong. The truth is that we all have better and worse times, according to the weather and the state of our finances. Students are no different in this, and because they are in close proximity to one another they usually manage to reflect the moods of those around them. Be aware that your planning should take into consideration these highs and lows in terms of the amount of material to be covered in a particular length of time and the importance of motivations.

CHILD DEVELOPMENT
DURING THE YEAR

Another time rhythm that is different in education from the business world is that of child development. The plant manager can sit down and plot his product from raw materials to finished over a certain period. Your product, the educated child, is not produced in a smooth, predictable sequence. While we know quite a bit about the physical development of a human being from neonate to adult, we are still not sure about the accompanying psychological changes and how to effect them. You will teach children whose learning seems as jagged as an outline of the Alps. One day Marvin will know how to do exchange, the next he will seem blank on the process. You will teach some children who will grow twice as much mentally and physically in one year as others in the same class. You will teach some children who will appear to have learned nothing and see them suddenly begin to respond for no apparent reason.

One of the most difficult tasks in teaching is to allow for the differences that exist even in the most "homogeneous" class. Sometimes those differences widen or narrow during the year. Children simply do not develop in the same way and at the same rate. Perhaps a child is ready to learn, and perhaps she or he is not. Remember this in planning for your school year and be adaptable enough to accept the pace that will be set for you by the stages of development within the children of your class.

EXERCISE

Find your lesson plan book and the material from the Human Survival course. Superimpose over your time line the highs and lows suggested for various months above. Would this change the way you would teach the course? How?

DOG DAYS

Because the school year has its ups and downs, you will find yourself sometimes under more stress and strain than others. You will have days when neither you nor your students will appear to be making headway. You will have days when you and your students will seem mired in an endless struggle. Everyone has this experience, and it is not peculiar to education. What makes it different for teachers, though, is that you are engaged in an enterprise where a number of people are working together in a limited space for relatively long periods of time. Most people have some privacy in their jobs. You must always perform before a group.

There are several ways to help beat the blues. First, you should be aware that it's perfectly normal to have them even if you are a usually optimistic person. Second, you can forestall them by being prepared, with a change-of-pace lesson or a change of environment. Third, when the dark days of March are upon you, remember that your mood is temporary. June will come.

ABSENCES AND LATENESSES

Some teachers escape the cumulative effect of dog days through a day of absence for "R&R." The whole area of lateness and absence, however, is a very touchy one in terms of professional responsibility. Some teachers are hardly ever absent. Others are out frequently. Some teachers have "traffic problems" day after day. Others arrive early as a rule.

Most school systems indicate in the teacher's contract their rules on absence and lateness. Usually a teacher will be allowed a certain number of absences each year and will be able to accumulate unused absence days up to a maximum, such as ninety days. Usually a teacher will be allowed some lateness with a reasonable excuse, but at a certain point may be docked or have time taken from sick leave.

Aside from the strictly practical matter of your absence or lateness, you should consider the problems that may occur because of your not being in the classroom. Some areas find it difficult to hire substitutes, and even capable substitutes will not be able to teach your class as you would. You will discover if you are out of school for several days that it may take an inordinate amount of work to get your class back on the track. They and you have been un-sequenced.

No one will ever ask you to come to school when you are not fit to work. And it may be very true that a day off can do wonders for your viewpoint and send you back to the classroom ready to rassle the learning tiger. But if you find that the only solution to your problems in school seems to be escape, then you may want to reconsider your choice of job. You may be working at the wrong level, in the wrong school, or in the wrong field.

LEGAL MATTERS

Every state has a body of school law, some similar and some quite different from others. In general it is unnecessary for the teacher to be aware of or concerned about the law except for two instances. Those are accidents and tenure. And during every school year these matters will become important to some teachers.

An accident in a school can be something that happens to the teacher or something that happens to the student. It is a good idea to have a set routine to follow which applies in either case. Some schools already have a procedure. If yours does not, it would be wise to take the following steps.

1.   Take care of the accident victim as well as you can and send for help to your supervisor immediately. Try to make the person as comfortable as possible. Do not move anyone, but do help the victim who insists on moving himseif or herself.

2.   Have someone write down the exact time and place of the accident and the names of any witnesses. If possible, ask witnesses to sit down and write an account of what they saw.

3.   Write an account of the accident yourself. This is particularly important if it occurs in a classroom where you are the person in charge.

4.   Find out if the school or system requires that a special form be filled out within a particular number of hours after the accident. Have a supervisor help you with the form to make sure it is accurate.

5.   If you are the accident victim, ask your supervisor to find out what your rights are in connection with absences and/or sick pay and job assurance. If there are special forms to be filled out, be sure you have been given them.

Another area of legal concern to some teachers is the matter of tenure. Tenure means the secured right to a job. It is different from seniority, which is simply the length of time in a position. Some systems grant tenure automatically after a certain period of satisfactory teaching, from one to five years according to locale. In other systems tenure is not automatic. Each teacher in that case is considered individually and the record is checked not only for satisfactory classroom performance but also absences, latenesses, and other factors. Tenure can be important to you, but the only way you will know what applies in your case is to ask. There may be district circulars that give details. If not, your supervisor or the payroll secretary in your school should be able to tell you the facts. If you are a new teacher in the school or system, it is a good idea to know what your procedures and rights regarding tenure are.

PERSONNEL MATTERS

Be alert during the school year to anything that arrives in your school mailbox with the heading of your school board. You may receive notices about health insurance, for instance. In larger systems there may be a choice of insurance to which you are entitled but only a specific number of days in which you can change plans. There may be notices changing regulations for accreditation or for moving from one salary step to another. Many of these notices appear to be written by a wizened Victorian lawyer at a rolltop desk. You may not understand what they say. If so, be brave enough to seek help even when you feel foolish. You are not a trained legal mind but a teacher. And you are entitled to understand any conditions which may change your salary or fringe benefits.

EXERCISE

Write down at least six questions you might have on absence, lateness, accidents, tenure, fringe benefits, and accreditation. If you are teaching now, go ask them of your supervisor or the school secretary. If you are not teaching now, clip them inside your lesson plan book for future reference.

HOLIDAYS AND VACATIONS

The school year does include a number of holidays and a goodly block of vacation time. What you do with these periods of relaxation can influence your classroom performance immeasurably. It may be wise for you to plan ahead to make sure that you experience that renewal of purpose so necessary to teachers.

The feeling of renewal is necessary to everyone, of course. Its importance to teachers, though, is accepted by anyone who has ever spent 180-plus days in a classroom. During the school year even the least dedicated teacher is bound closely to the educational fortunes of a number of children. From the time a teacher steps inside the school door, no matter how many preparation periods that person has, there is really no relief from the responsibilities of Jack and Jean and Gil. Most teachers take work home day after day, spend time outside of school hours contacting parents, attending workshops and advanced college courses, meeting with parents and community, polishing skills and knowledge through professional associations and reading. You will find yourself wrung dry sometimes by the intensity of the demands of your job. If you do not do something about it during your holidays and vacations, you may well become psychologically depressed and physically run-down.

What you do in your spare time is, of course, your own business. One person's woodworking is another's chores. Whatever you do, though, should be something for yourself. As a teacher the major part of your life will be centered around what other people do. In your privacy, one way to renew is to cater to that part of you which is not engaged in teaching. Some teachers find sports relaxing. Others prefer hobbies dependent on working with your hands. Still more find hobbies removed from education worthwhile.

Many teachers use holidays and vacations for travel. This movement away from an area where you are literally pent up in one place for long working time has two benefits. The first, change of scene, is obvious. The second is that wherever you travel you may find something that can be utilized in your teaching. Educators use the summer both to travel and to gain more college credits. There are a number of agencies that arrange trips that carry some kind of learning benefit, in Europe,

Asia, or Africa. Many professional organizations arrange special charters or group tours. The carriers themselves, ship or airplane, often offer something special for teachers.

It is a sad fact of teaching life that for some people vacations cannot be wasted on relaxation. It often becomes necessary, especially for a family breadwinner, to take a second job. If you are able to do so and must work, it might be well to consider a job totally unrelated to teaching. Although some educators run summer camps, day-care centers, or recreation programs, most discover that there is little relief in the type of work so closely akin to the classroom experience. You may find it of more psychological value and just as wise financially to contact a temporary employment service or find a part-time position in sales. At the least, such work is a change in pace for you and a glimpse of the way the rest of the world lives.

Whether you are able to travel or must work or, à la Pangloss, tend your own garden, be sure to provide yourself with some mental change from your role as teacher. Only then will you welcome September with the same excitement as the first graders with their brand new lunchboxes.

SUMMARY

1. The school year is shorter, more intense and has different patterns than the business year.
2. During the school year be knowledgeable about the dog days, absence and lateness policies, legal matters, and personnel rules.
3. During holidays and vacations, try to change your mental or physical occupation in order to renew yourself.

HOMEWORK

Plan now for your next vacation. If you can travel then, decide where you will go, how long and how much you can spend, how you will get there, and what you will do when you get there. If you must work, read the classified ads of your local newspaper and decide what occupations interest you most for which you are qualified. Make notes on your plans and put them in your lesson plan book under March.

CHAPTER THIRTEEN

LIFE AFTER THREE

WHEN CAN I BE ME?

AIMS

1. To realize that the general public regards teaching as a profession, not a job
2. To know what implications particular outside activities may have
3. To consider professional options after 3 p.m.

MOTIVATION

Mr. J has just run out of salt at 9:30 Sunday night. He throws on the first clothes he can grab and dashes to the market before its 10 p.m. closing. Naturally he runs into Candida and her mother, who smiles coolly and moves pointedly away. He overhears her saying to Candida from the next aisle, "That scruffy man is your bio teacher? He's wearing jeans with holes in them." Mr. J feels like orating but instead takes his dignity and purchase to the checkout counter.

TEACHING:
JOB OR PROFESSION?

Whether you agree or not, most people believe that teaching is a profession. And the gap between a profession and a job can open pitfalls which you may not foresee. Indeed this is a controversy within education itself where only in recent years in some areas have practitioners belonged to a "union" rather than an "association." Whatever your attitude may be, you will have to deal with the attitude which prevails around you both in and out of school. And it is still true that the majority do not associate time cards and contract working conditions with teaching.

There are advantages, of course, in being regarded as a professional. If you as a teacher are a professional, then it should be taken for granted that you need time for professional activities, after school and during vacations. If you are a professional, you have a certain amount of subliminal authority that is recognized in people's dealings with you. If you are a professional, then you are automatically considered better trained and more highly qualified than those in "jobs."

Certainly those members of the public who set up salary schedules for teachers consider yours a profession. In education your financial advancement is usually dependent on two factors—length of service and completion of advanced courses. Payment of salary is also based on professional rather than occupational time spent. You receive your money not on an hourly rate but on a yearly basis. That year is ordinarily a 12-month one also, rather than a 9-month one. Even part-time substitutes are generally not paid by the hour but by the day.

In addition, teaching is regarded as a profession by government. Each state and some cities have specific requirements for obtaining a teaching license. Some areas have various levels of teaching licenses, according to college credits and experience. These licensing qualifications place teaching on the same level as the medical and legal professions.

Pay and licensing requirements, however, are not the areas which will have the most impact on you in this job-versus-profession debate. It is the public's view of your position for which you will have to prepare. To the general community your job is not finished when you leave the school. Since to them you are a professional, you must expect to be a teacher on the street, at the movies, in stores, at parties, and at the end of a telephone in your own home. Students and parents will greet you, consult you, admire you, and deprecate you in your activities outside of school. Perfect strangers, on hearing that you are a teacher, will freely give you their opinions and solutions to educational problems that you did not even know existed. You will be expected to give time, money, and energy to others' worthy causes because you are a teacher. If you stray from the community's moral path, your error will be worse.

Some teachers solve this problem by living in an area other than the one where they work, although this may be against regulations in some communities. Others learn to ignore the unnecessary intrusions on their personal lives and accept those that can't be avoided with mannerly grace. A very few become deliberately outré from sheer defiance, although this takes a remarkably strong character. What your adaptation is to these realities must be your individual decision. You will, though, have to make a decision about what impact you will permit teaching to have on your life off school grounds.

EXERCISE

Divide a paper into two columns headed Profession and Job. Give yourself three minutes to list as many teacher job characteristics as you can in each column. Which column was easier to fill? What does that indicate in your attitude toward your own position?

YOUR PERSONAL LIFE
AS A TEACHER

Your activities outside of school, then, are bound to come under some scrutiny unless you spend all your time inside the four walls of your home. There are, though, certain categories of activity which will probably receive the most attention from the public at large. They are your personal relationships, your behavior and dress, your politics, and the whole wide area of professional activities. In all of these categories you are entitled to certain privacy rights by the constitution, court decisions, and laws. On the other hand, in some communities life can become extremely uncomfortable for you, if not downright nasty, when you do not recognize that you are, in a sense, a public figure.

One factor you should realize is that your friends, your family, and your lovers in most communities will be considered an extension of yourself. Parents, rightly or wrongly, feel that their children's teachers provide a moral as well as educational climate. If you do not agree with the ethos of those around you and make this obvious through your associations with others, you can be in for rough weather. Those who prefer to live in a way different from their neighbors have the choice of discretion or of being obvious. If you believe that you cannot compromise your way of life by using discretion, then you should be careful to know the community in which you work. For example, if you live with someone to whom you are not married and it is an obvious sexual relationship, you may be accepted in some towns and cities, rejected in others. This is an important consideration for you in choosing a teaching position.

BEHAVIOR AND DRESS

The way you behave and/or dress may be subject to criticism from others, also, simply because you are a teacher. Though the day is long past when female teachers needed dresses to the ankles and male teachers had to wear a jacket and tie, some communities may evince strong feelings against unusual dress. Your out-of-school behavior, especially as regards alcohol and drugs, may also be noted. If you are convicted of law-breaking such as drunken driving, you may legally, in some places, be fired. If you are arrested for a violation of law, some systems may suspend you. And even if your activities are not illegal but do run counter to the prevailing mores, you can find your position eroded in terms of the attitude of students or the school's administration.

Luckily we are no longer living in the years when teachers were required in some places to take loyalty oaths. Indeed teachers may be among the most active political groups in the country. You as an individual, though, may find that certain political activities do not sit well in some areas. It is quite obvious that a social studies teacher who is an avowed communist may be open to community criticism. It is not so obvious that a teacher active in an environmental pressure group may be objectionable to a community dependent on one local heavy industry.

These are unfortunate facts of life for teachers. One person's right may be another person's wrong. And because you have intimate contact with the young of a particular community, when your views run counter to that community you may have a rough time. Of course, you feel that you should have the right to live as you please. Technically you are correct. In practice this may not be so.

EXERCISE

Somewhere in everyone's life there has been a teacher who made an indelible impression for good or bad. Think of such a teacher you have encountered and try to remember anything you knew about that person outside the classroom. Did that person's outside life make any difference to you or your parents in your attitudes? From what type of community do you come?

PROFESSIONAL ACTIVITIES AVAILABLE TO YOU

As a teacher you have the opportunity to engage in professional activities after regular school hours. Most teachers find this a rewarding part of education. The options available to you are generally three: extra-curricular activities with students, advanced studies, and participation in some professional organization.

Extracurricular activities

Most secondary schools, both junior and senior high schools, offer students a variety of after-school activities. This is the obvious thought that occurs when one mentions the extra-curricular. If you are a new teacher, however, and teacher-advisors are paid in your system, it is unlikely that you will be involved here since seniority is usually observed. If the work is voluntary, your services will probably be welcome. Perhaps you can even create a paid job for yourself if you have specialized experience or knowledge, such as expertise in developing a new sports team or club. There is also the possibility that you might apply for a grant from a governmental agency for a worthwhile after-school project, like a local teen center. In addition, in your system there may be remedial or adult education classes in the afternoon, at night, or during summer vacation.

To some teachers the thought of working with students and/or teaching outside of school hours is not attractive. To others the chance to have a more casual relationship with children and encourage involvement in a favorite sport or activity may be well worth the time. If you are interested in after-school advising, teaching or working, you should explore the possibilities by talking to other teachers and to administrators. At the very least, this type of activity is something possible to add to the experience section of your resume.

Advanced studies

As noted before, most salary advancement in teaching includes requirements for further college credits. Some systems are specific. You must take a first-aid course or a human-relations course in order to advance to a particular step. Others require only a specific number of credits without limits on subject area. Most systems also pay an extra premium for an accumulated number of credits over and above the basic degrees. Holding a doctorate in some school systems can put hard cash in your pocket. In some areas of the country there are arrangements made between school systems and local universities which result in a reduced rate or scholarship status for employed teachers studying after school or in the summer. All this adds up to a basic reason for continuing your studies while you are in teaching.

Of course, unless you are informed otherwise, there is no reason why you must stick to education courses in your post-graduate studies. You can use this time to explore other interests or begin courses that can advance you even more, in school administration and supervision, for instance. You may become attracted by another subject area or grade level, and you can use this studying time to develop a specialization.

It also makes good sense to continue your studies simply because you are a teacher. You will find you have a keener awareness of methods and practices when you sit in the student's seat part-time. And workshop courses designed for current teachers can also help you overcome the basic problems everyone encounters in their first few years of teaching.

Professional organizations

Whether you enjoy it or not, as a teacher you belong to a specific group. And teachers banded together in a professional organization can and have made differences, not only in basic working conditions, but in the broad field of education. Teachers' organizations have sponsored research and experimentation in how children learn and how they can learn better. Teachers' groups have been instrumental in establishing grassroots teacher centers where there can be an exchange of ideas and practices that are current and effective. Teachers' organizations have an effect on education through local, state and national lobbying. You may not agree with specific actions or philosophy of a particular teachers' organization, but there are a variety open to you.

There is probably a specialized teachers' organization for your field, also. You may want to belong to a city or state group whose professional interests coincide with your own in English, social studies, middle school, bilingual education and on ad infinitum. Every participant is welcome in a vibrant group. Although you may feel inexperienced in your teaching, you will learn quickly that simply belonging to a professional association can expand your knowledge enormously.

Most larger teachers' groups have conferences. If you can take the time and money necessary to attend, you will learn even more. And it is possible sometimes to obtain a partial reimbursement of time and/or money from your system. Your participation in a conference can be a plus for your school.

SUMMARY

1. Be prepared to be regarded as a professional with subsequent attention to your out-of-school activities.
2. If your personal life, behavior, dress or politics is noticeably different, expect some reaction from the community.
3. Use your out-of-school hours in worthwhile professional activities.

HOMEWORK

Consult your local library for a list of those teacher oganizations active in your city or state. Write a letter to at least two of them for membership information. If possible, choose organizations whose publications you have seen. For help in locating some of the many organizations available, see the list below.

Teacher Organizations

American Alliance for Health, Physical Education and Recreation
1201 16th Street NW
Washington, D.C. 20036

American Federation of Teachers
11 DuPont Circle NW
Washington, D.C. 20036

Council for Exceptional Children
1920 Association Drive
Reston, Virginia 22091

International Reading Association
P.O. Box 8139
800 Barkdale Road
Newark, Delaware 19711

Modern Language Association of America
62 Fifth Avenue
New York, N.Y. 10011

Music Teachers National Association
408 Carew Tower
Cincinnati, Ohio 45202

National Art Educators Association
1916 Association Drive
Reston, Virginia 22091

National Association of Bilingual Education
BESL Center
100 Franklin Street
New Holland, Pennsylvania 17557

National Association for Education of Young Children
1834 Connecticut Avenue
Washington, D.C. 20009

National Council of Teachers of English
1111 Kenyon Road
Urbana, Illinois 61801

National Council of Teachers of Math
1906 Association Drive
Reston, Virginia 22091

National Education Association
1201 16th Street NW
Washington, D.C. 20036

National Middle School Association
P. O. Box 968
Fairborn, Ohio 45324

National Science Teachers Association
1742 Connecticut Avenue NW
Washington, D.C. 20009

Office Education Association
1120 Morse Road
Columbus, Ohio 43229

Teachers of English to Speakers of Other Languages
School of Languages and Linguistics
Georgetown University
Washington, D.C. 20057

CHAPTER FOURTEEN

MONDAY MORNING

WHAT IN THE WORLD
AM I DOING HERE?

AIMS

1. To understand why teachers feel stress.
2. To understand how to deal with stress in yourself and others.
3. To consider why you are a teacher.

MOTIVATION

Ms. R has been teaching for six months, and there is something wrong. She likes the students and her job, but everything is stale. Every day seems like a Monday. She simply can't think of anything new to do in the classroom, and the school day plods along as fast as polo in a pool of molasses. Vitamins don't help. There's no one to complain to, and she wouldn't know what to complain about anyhow. After all, isn't she doing what she's always wanted to do? Why then does life seem like an endless chore?

**HANDLING YOUR
OWN STRESS**

Only in recent years has teaching been recognized as stress-causing work. The spectrum from mild depression to nervous breakdown is usually represented somewhere in every school system. Of course every job, except perhaps that of mattress tester, produces stress at one time or another. But teachers often find themselves under stress for several reasons. You should recognize these reasons in order to deal with it.

First, teaching is a lonely job, oddly enough. Although you are rarely alone while working, you will probably feel isolated at times. Your students are not good confidantes. The administration is, after all, your "boss," and you may hesitate to admit your concerns to a supervisor. Other teachers are generally busy, and, if they are more experienced, you may not want to discuss your shortcomings with them. Your family and friends really cannot understand your position because they generally are not familiar with the classroom situation.

In addition to loneliness you as teacher may find yourself under stress because of the pressures. While there are other more deadline-oriented jobs, they usually have some periods of relief. Teaching means being under constant pressure. There is no day when you can sit back and let matters take their own course in your classroom. You must work and work intelligently every minute that you are with students, and that is the major part of your working day.

Teaching is also stressful because you cannot always and sometimes rarely see the actual results of your work. You will see manifestations of your work, in discussions, homework, tests, and responses from students. But most of the time you will never really know if you have accomplished anything unless you are lucky enough to teach a subject such as English as a second language. The product of your labors, an educated child, is an amalgam of learning in which your individual contribution may not even be apparent. Much has been made of teacher accountability, but little concrete measurement of teaching is yet possible.

To make matters worse from the standpoint of stress, students are constantly changing. The best of teachers cannot predict exactly what will be the success of a particular lesson for each student. Children grow at different rates and have varying needs at different times. A teacher must adapt to this fact, and this need for continual flexibility can produce stress in itself.

HANDLING STRESS
IN OTHERS

Part of a teacher's classroom reality is dealing with stress not only in oneself but in others. There are no easy answers to the problem of one's own stress. The best are ones you discover individually, but there are at least three general actions you can take that may help.

As a beginning, help to alleviate your own pressures by finding some way to verbalize them. Although your friends and family may not be able to offer solutions, or even completely understand your problems, their sympathetic ears will allow you to blow off steam. If you have someone within the school whom you trust, talking out the strains you are experiencing can relieve you. Even if there is absolutely no one in whom you are able or willing to confide, you can still get a kind of verbal catharsis through writing. Somehow the act of expressing your tensions, even if you tear up the paper later, can give you surcease.

Next, stress can sometimes be relieved by doing something different. You may accomplish this in or out of the classroom. In the classroom, try redecorating the walls, changing the furniture or experimenting with a new procedure in class routine, books or teaching practice. Outside the classroom, go somewhere you have never been before, change your hair style, take up a new sport or hobby, write a fan letter to someone you admire, or fire off a protest to the newspaper. The mere act of doing something can often act as a safety valve for your feelings, particularly when your reaction to stress is depression.

One of the best ways to combat tension is to recognize it as such and accept it as a normal reaction. Everyone suffers from nervous headaches, stomach cramps, and the "blahs" at one psychosomatic time or another. You are an average child of nature when you become cranky, edgy and quarrelsome under pressure. Once you begin to understand that what is happening to you is par in most teachers' lives, you should realize that these feelings are momentary not momentous. Being ready to take arms against your sea of troubles can turn it into a millpond.

Steering your own way through times of stress may be

simpler than helping others under pressure, particularly when they are others whose tension makes them turn on you. The teachers who feel that their classroom troubles are another's fault, the paperbound and harried administrator, the student who has troubles at home that spill into your room, are all people whom you will probably meet. There are two ways of dealing with others whose stress has an effect on your teaching life.

One is to invoke the "there but for the grace of God go I" viewpoint. You have or will have suffered from stress yourself. It behooves you to remember this when you see others straining, and to be sympathetic. Realize, too, that your reaction to the other person may aggravate the situation. Even when you are being treated unfairly by someone under tension, keeping your cool at least temporarily may ameliorate the problem.

There are times, however, when you may see someone under so much stress that your sympathy or kindness can mean little if anything. In this case, it is your responsibility to urge that the person receive help, preferably professional. If you feel your advice on getting that help may be listened to, give it to the person under stress. If you feel that someone else needs to talk to the person, then find that someone else, whether it is a member of the person's family, another teacher, a guidance counselor, or your supervisor. If the person is a teacher, you cannot in conscience just "let things go." Teachers have intimate contact with children. Your first duty is toward the children who can be affected by a teacher under extreme pressures.

Most of the time, the stress you will be dealing with in yourself and others is temporary. It arrives and departs as quickly as a summer storm. Remember that you can do something about it, and you will be halfway along the road to resolution.

EXERCISE

Imagine yourself under stress as a classroom teacher. What specific things in terms of your own life and interests, could you do to relieve it? Write them down and tape them in front of your lesson plan book.

WHY TEACH?

For the fifth day in a row, the weather forecasts temperatures over 90° F (32° C). Ms. D can feel her dress beginning to stick to her back. Reading Group Alpha is droning out the words of an inane story. There is a smell of sour milk from the morning snacks. Next door in Ms. B's room the sounds are different. The usual range from student murmurs to high-pitched scolding has given way to loud shouting. Suddenly Ms. D's door opens and her neighbor almost falls into the room. There are tears running down her cheeks as she shouts, "I can't stand it any longer."

The class watches in awed silence as Ms. D guides the other teacher to a chair. "Run and get Mr. O," she tells a student. "No, no," cries Mrs. B, "I'm untenured. They'll fire me." Her sobs become noisier. "All right," Ms. D answers, "Let's walk over to the teachers' room where you can have some privacy. Class, I'm leaving the door open, and I expect everyone to behave as if I were here."

In the teachers' room, bathing Ms. B's face with paper towels wrung out in cold water, Ms. D listens to a breathless list of problems, physical, mental, and educational. As she leaves Ms. B slumped exhaustedly on the room's sleazy couch, Ms. D can feel the beginnings of a headache. When she walks into her room she is just in time to intercept John's spitball present to Ellen. As she looks around the agitated class, Ms. D says to herself, "How in the world did I get here?"

Aside from tension, teachers may also experience great sweeps of insecurity. Classroom life does not lend itself to calm meditation. There is always something that must be done at this moment. It is not unusual to be brought up short by a sudden bewilderment as to the purpose of your life.

Whether you have chosen teaching for idealistic or realistic reasons, you are bound to encounter a time when you question that decision. Whatever you expect from teaching may not materialize. Time was when the bottom line was the security of a job because teachers were in great demand. Later there were the perquisites of much time off and a fairly acceptable salary.

For teachers new to the classroom there was always the hope of becoming an instant Mr. Chips or Miss Jean Brodie. All of these attractions have been proved false to teacher after teacher in every school system in the country.

Why then do teachers continue opening the windows, shutting the windows, writing lesson plans, washing blackboards, totalling attendance, attending faculty meetings, and taking part in all the rest of the endless activities that make up a teacher's day, week, month, and year?

Some people remain in teaching because they do not know what else to do. Some people remain in teaching because they are planning another career and meanwhile it pays. And some people remain in teaching simply because they like the act of teaching. They look forward to that once-in-a-while feeling of having accomplished some part of a student's education. They accept the dross of the classroom in the expectation of one golden gleam of interest in a child's eye. They anticipate their successes in dealing with their often failures. Even in a temporary insecurity, they know that there is purpose and meaning for them in what they do.

If you are determined, you will know that, too.

SUMMARY

1. Understand that all teachers feel stress because of loneliness, pressure, lack of obvious results and the need for constant adaptability.
2. Deal with stress in yourself by verbalizing it, doing something different or simply recognizing it.
3. Deal with stress in others by realizing it could be you. In extreme cases try to see that the person receives professional help.
4. Know why you are a teacher because that knowledge is necessary to your daily school life.

HOMEWORK

Read the Blue Monday Checklist below. Fill in the blanks, cut it out and put it along with your own stress relief list in the front of your lesson plan book.

Blue Monday Checklist

I am a teacher because_____

_____

If I am edgy or irritable more than one day with my students, I will:

_____ move my desk from one side of the room to the other

_____ do a change-of-pace lesson

_____ check the Teacher's Calendar and change the room decorations

_____ show a film or filmstrip in class

_____ plan a trip with a class

_____ plan a project with a homeroom

_____ enroll in a course outside of my own field that interests me

_____ buy something new to wear

_____ call up my parents/friends/other relatives and tell them that I'm feeling blue

_____ plan a trip for my next vacation

_____ read a classic in my field

_____ go out to dinner in a new restaurant

_____ go to a museum/play/movie that I haven't seen

_____ write a list of my good qualities

_____ begin a journal

_____ learn a new sport or game

_____ buy records to learn a new language

_____ clean out my closets (in school and at home)

INDEX

ABOUT
THE AUTHOR

Margaret Martin Maggs' present position involves coordinating the activities of teachers, 500 students, para-professionals, and parents in a secondary school bilingual program, with a 75 percent Hispanic population, for the New York City Board of Education. Born in Houston, Texas, she has lived all over the United States and now resides in New York City. Ms. Maggs is a second generation teacher with sixteen years of experience, who spent twelve years writing for advertising and publicity. She is a member of Phi Delta Kappa, married and the mother of twin sons. Ms. Maggs is currently conducting workshops on teacher survival in the classroom. *The Classroom Survival Book* is her third book.